VEDANTA PHILOSOPHY
SELF-KNOWLEDGE
(ATMA-JNANA)

VEDANTA PHILOSOPHY

SELF-KNOWLEDGE

(ATMA-JNANA)

SWAMI ABHEDANANDA

GYAN

Published by

GYAN

Gyan Publishing House
5, Ansari Road
Daryaganj, New Delhi-110002
Phone: 011-47034999, 9811692060
E-mail: books@gyanbooks.com

Distribution Network
gyanbooks.com
India, USA, Canada, UK, Australia

ISBN: 978-93-6920-492-2 (HB)

First Published, 1905

2nd Impression 2025

Printed at: Gyan Press, Delhi.

VEDANTA PHILOSOPHY SELF-KNOWLEDGE
Author: SWAMI ABHEDANANDA

SWÂMI ABHEDÂNANDA.

VEDANTA PHILOSOPHY

SELF-KNOWLEDGE

(ATMA-JNANA)

BY

SWAMI ABHEDANANDA

Author of "India and her People," "How to be a Yogi," "Divine Heritage of Man," "Reincarnation," etc.

THIRD EDITION

PUBLISHED BY

THE VEDANTA SOCIETY

WEST CORNWALL, CONN.

To

THE LOTUS FEET

OF

BHAGAVÂN SRI RÂMAKRISHNA

MY DIVINE GURU

BY

WHOSE GRACE

THE BLISS OF SELF-KNOWLEDGE

IS REALIZED

PREFACE.

In this age of scepticism and materialism few people care to know their real Self, which is Divine and immortal. But the knowledge of the true Self has always been the principal theme of the philosophy and religion of Vedanta. Even in its most ancient writings, the Upanishads, which form portions of the Vedic Scriptures, we find how earnestly Self-knowledge or Atma-jnâna was sought after and extolled. The great inspired seers mentioned in these Upanishads discovered and taught that knowledge of the Self lies at the root of all knowledge, whether of science, philosophy or religion. Every sincere seeker after knowledge, therefore, who desires intellectual, moral or spiritual development, must first learn to discriminate between spirit and matter, soul and body, and then realize the all-knowing Divine Self who is the eternal foundation of the universe.

CONTENTS.

"Matter or object is related to spirit or subject; and the subject or spirit is equally related to the object or matter. If there were no object, there would be no subject; and if there were no subject, there would be no object. For on either side alone nothing could be achieved."

Kaushitaki Upanishad, III, 8.

SPIRIT AND MATTER.

Spirit and matter have always been subjects for discussion in science, philosophy and religion. The great thinkers of all countries have tried their best to understand the true meanings of these two terms and to establish their mutual relation. The two words have various synonyms, such as ego and non-ego, subject and object, mind and matter. Scientists and philosophers have advanced many theories from time to time to explain their ideas and conceptions about them and have arrived at different conclusions. Some say that spirit or mind or ego is the cause of matter, while others reverse the relation and believe that matter is the cause of spirit or mind or ego. These conclusions have given foundation to the various explanations of the universe, which can be classified under three heads,—the spiritualistic or idealistic, the materialistic, and the monistic theories. The spiritualistic or idealistic theory claims that spirit or mind is the creator of matter and energy, hence of all material objects; and it denies the existence of matter as distinct and separate from the mode or condition of spirit or mind. The materialistic theory, on the contrary, maintains that matter produces spirit, mind, ego or subject.

There have been many idealistic or spiritualistic philosophers in different countries at different times. In India, Greece, Germany, and England have arisen a number of idealists like Bishop Berkeley, who have denied the existence of the external world and also of matter as an entity separate from mental ideas. Modern Christian Science, which teaches that there is no such thing as matter but that everything is mind, has been built upon this idealistic doctrine of Bishop Berkeley and other philosophers of the same school. In America it is new, because the nation is new. America has not yet produced any great idealistic philosopher.

The materialistic theory of the universe, on the other hand, is maintained by a large majority of the scientists, physicists, chemists, medical practitioners and the evolutionists of the present time. They try to deduce everything from matter, and claim that it is the cause of mind, ego or spirit. Although there are thousands and millions of people all over the world who advocate this theory and call themselves materialists, still very few can define the term matter and give a clear idea of what they understand by it.

What is matter? Has anybody ever seen matter? This question can be asked of the materialists. Do we see matter? No. We see color. Is color the same as matter? No. It is a quality. Where does it exist? An uneducated man may think that the color of a flower, as perceived, exists in the flower. But the physiologists explain that the color which is perceived does not exist as such in the flower, but that it is a sensation caused by a certain order of vibrations coming in contact with our consciousness through the medium of the optic nerves. This may seem strange, but it is true. The perception of color is a compound effect produced by vibrations of ether, which, entering through the eyes, create another set of vibrations in the brain cells; and these vibrations, when translated by the conscious entity, are called sensations. Color, therefore, is the result of the blending of the objective and subjective elements. It is the product of the combination of that which comes from the outside world and that which is given by the subjective or mental activities. Thus we can understand that color does not rest in the flower; but it depends upon the retinæ, optic nerves and brain cells as well, so it cannot be the same as matter.

Similarly we may ask: Is sound which we

hear the same as matter? No. It is the result of a certain kind of vibration plus the conscious activity of the mind. If you go to sleep, the vibration of sound will enter through your ears and be carried through the auditory nerves into the brain cells, but you will not hear it, because the percipient mind is not there to translate the vibration into the sensation of sound. Sound, therefore, is not the same as matter. In the same manner it can be shown that the other senses do not give us any information about that which we call matter. Then we ask: What is matter? John Stewart Mill defines matter as the "permanent possibility of sensation," and mind as the "permanent possibility of feeling." Are we better off after hearing this definition? On the contrary, it is more confusing. The whole difficulty lies in the word "possibility." It means, matter is that which permanently makes sensation possible, and mind or spirit is that which permanently makes feeling possible; or, in other words matter is that which can be permanently felt or perceived, that which is the object of feeling; and spirit is that which can permanently feel or perceive, that which is the subject of feeling.

That which permanently makes sensation possible can never be revealed by the senses, for the senses are no more than open doors for our sensations. All that we can predicate of matter is that it causes sensations. When we try to know its nature *per se*, or any particulars concerning it, our senses do not help us. The eyes are only instrumental in perceiving the sensation of color, the ears of sound, nostrils of odor. Our perception of the external world is limited by these sense powers, and all sensations are either direct or indirect results of our sense activities. Although we know that matter is something which exists in space and time and causes various sensations, still we cannot see or touch it. That which corresponds to the name "matter" will always remain intangible.

We may touch a chair, a piece of wood or gold, but we cannot touch matter by itself. This is very curious. Gold or stone is not matter, but it is that which is produced by matter. Matter appears as wood or stone.

It may be interesting to know the history of the term matter. This word is derived from the Latin *materies*, meaning "stuff," and it was originally used in the sense of the solid wood of a tree or a timber for building. Gradually a generalized concept was formed which meant anything substantial out of which some other thing was fashioned. When a wooden statue was made, the form was distinguished from the substance wood or *materies*. Here it was still wood. But when a statue was made of stone or metal it was still called *materies*. Thus the name *materies* signified the substance out of which something was shaped or fashioned. Gradually when the question arose, "What was the substance out of which this world was made?" the answer was *materies* or matter. So the word matter does not mean any definite thing. It is used for that unknown substance out of which the known objects of perception are formed. Here ends the literal and real meaning of the term. Matter can be used in the sense of any unknown substance which lies at the bottom or foundation of some form or object. For instance, in our ordinary conversation we use this word in such expressions as "What is the matter?" "It does not matter," "Important matter," "Decaying matter."

In science and philosophy, however, matter is that unknown substance out of which all phenomenal forms are fashioned. It is beyond sense perception, yet it underlies all the objects of the universe. It is not the same as space or time, but it fills space, manifests itself in time, and cannot be limited by the category of causality. All these ideas are included in the meaning of the term matter. When we think of that substance of which the universe is the appearance, we imagine that it is vast, immense, marvellous and possessed of wonderful powers, which are constantly changing. But what is matter? Is it one or many? It is one. We cannot say that it is many. Herbert Spencer says: "Our conception of matter, reduced to its simplest shape, is that of coëxistent positions that offer resistance, as contrasted with our conception of space in which the coëxistent positions offer no resistance." (First Principles, p. 140.) Let us understand the difference between space and matter. Space is extension offering no resistance, but that which offers resistance and lies in space is matter. He also states: "Of these two inseparable elements, the resistance is primary and the extension is secondary." As, for example, when we touch something it resists, then we have an idea of resistance; but when we spread our hand that feeling of resistance extends also in space. Herbert Spencer says again: "Our experience of force is that out of which the idea of matter is built up. . . . That which opposes our muscular energy is immediately present to consciousness in the terms of force. Hence forces, standing in a certain correlation in space, form the whole content of matter." Furthermore, he adds: "Matter and motion, as we know them, are differently conditioned manifestations of force. They are the concretes built up from the contents of various mental relations." In order to feel resistance there must be present one who feels; and then the force that is felt is the primary cause which gives rise to the conception of matter.

Again, matter has not been created by anybody. No one has ever seen, nor can anyone imagine the creation of matter out of nothing or its total annihilation. According to modern science, matter in its true nature is a substance uncreatable and indestructible, that is, it was neither created out of nothing nor can it go back into nothing. There are various other definitions of matter.

Some physicists say that matter is "whatever possesses the property of gravitative attraction." But still this does not tell us its true nature. We can only say that there is some substance which responds to attractions. Ernst Haeckel, again, defines matter as "infinitely extended substance, and spirit as all-embracing energy of thought."

After studying these various definitions, we learn that matter is that substance of the universe which makes up the objective world, or that which can be perceived by the senses and cognized by the mind. It is always objective, and spirit or mind is always subjective, always the perceiver or cognizer of matter, the knower of the object. Now we can understand the difference,—spirit is the perceiver and knower, while matter is that which is perceived, sensed and known. The one is the subject and the other is the object. These two exist in relation to each other. The objective world or matter forms only one-half, while the other half is the subjective world or spirit. Therefore, the materialistic theory, which admits the existence of the object and denies the existence of spirit or mind or the subject, is onesided and imperfect. It ignores the fact that matter or object can only exist as related to the subject.

The materialistic theory is a logical blunder, because it is based upon a confusion between object and subject. It asserts that matter is objective, but at the same time it tries to show that it is also the cause of the subject, which can never be. "A" can never become "non-A." Materialism begins with the idea that matter is objective, and ends in attempting to prove that this objective something has become the subjective mind, spirit or ego. It first takes for granted that matter is that which is perceived, or the cause of sensations, then it gradually claims to show that it produces that which feels the sensations, which is self-contradictory and absurd.

As materialism is onesided and imperfect, so is the spiritualistic or idealistic theory of the world, which denies the existence of matter or object, and says that everything is mind. The theory of modern Christian Science,—that all is mind and that there is no matter, is as erroneous as the materialistic theory. Spirit or mind or ego, which is always the subject, can exist as perceiver or knower so long as there is an object of perception and of knowledge. If we admit the existence of one, that of the other is implied. Therefore, Goethe was correct in saying: "Matter cannot exist and be operative without spirit or spirit without matter."

The universal substance appears as possessing these two attributes of subject and object, of spirit, mind or ego and matter or non-ego. They are like the two modes of the one eternal substance, which is unknown and unknowable existence. It was called "Substantia" by Spinoza. Herbert Spencer calls it the "Unknowable." It is the same as "Ding an sich," or the transcendental thing-in-itself of Kant; Plato named it the "Good."

It is the "Over-Soul" of Emerson; while in Vedanta it is called "Brahman," the absolute substance of the universe, the infinite and eternal source of matter and mind, of object and subject. This substance is not many but one. All varieties of phenomena have come out of this one source, Brahman, and into it they will be reduced at the time of dissolution. It is the universal energy, the mother or producer of all forces. We know that all forces are related to one another and that they are, as modern science explains, the manifestations of the same eternal energy or the infinite substance. From this one source all mental and physical phenomena and material forces have come into existence, and have evolved into various forms and shapes.

This is monism. The monistic thinkers of the present age, like Ernst Haeckel and others, admit this one eternal substance as the source of mind, matter and all forces. They also accept the great truth which has always been taught by Vedanta that "From that infinite substance or Brahman, the Absolute Being, have evolved life-force or Prâna, mind, all the mental activities, and the sense powers, which are included in the meaning of the term "spirit" or subject on the one hand, and, on the other, space or ether, and all gaseous, liquid and solid objects which are understood by matter!" Matter in its simplest state can be reduced to the same infinite substance Brahman, which forms the background of mind or spirit. Therefore, Vedanta teaches that the eternal substance is both the material and the efficient cause of the universe. Although it is one, still it appears as many by its inscrutable power known in Vedanta as "Mâyâ."

This world is not made up of dead matter alone. It is not the product of the combination of those minute particles called atoms. Until lately the western physicists, chemists and other materialists believed that these atoms were indivisible units floating in the infinite space, attracting and repelling one another, mechanically producing the elements of nature and creating the phenomenal world. But now, through the application of electricity, J. J. Thomson, the great English scientist, has proved that the so-called indivisible atoms can be subdivided into still finer *electrons*, which are nothing but the force-centers of the ancient Hindu scientist. If atoms are made up of electrons, and electrons are but force-centers, where do they exist? They exist in that primordial ocean of infinite substance or Brahman, the receptacle of the eternal energy, which is in turn the mother of all forces. Thus, we can understand how matter and force are related to the one substance or Brahman. The objective side of that substance appears as matter, and the subjective side as spirit.

I have already said that it is a scientific truth that matter is indestructible and uncreatable; so is force. Matter and force can be transformed into various manifestations, but can never be destroyed. Now the question rises: If the one half of the world or objective matter and force be uncreatable and indestructible, then what is the nature of spirit? Is it creatable and destructible? If the objective half of the universe be uncreatable and indestructible, how can the other half, the subjective mind or spirit, be creatable and destructible? That is impossible. Spirit or mind in its simplest form is equally uncreated and indestructible. If matter or object be eternal, then the spirit or subject must also be eternal to make it possible for the object to be eternal. Who will know that matter and force are eternal, if the spirit or subject be not equally eternal? This point has been overlooked by most of the eminent thinkers and scientists of different countries. The eternality of matter and force or energy presupposes the eternality of spirit or mind. If the one falls, both will disappear. Therefore the ultimate analysis of spirit and matter shows that both are uncreatable, indestructible and eternal. If the one pole of a magnet be eternal, the other pole must necessarily be eternal. Furthermore, the neutral point where both meet must also be eternal. This universe is like a gigantic magnet, one pole of which is matter, and the other is spirit, while the neutral point is the absolute substance. For this reason these three, matter, spirit, and Brahman are eternal.

In Vedanta, spirit is called the Atman, the cognizer, the perceiver and the subject. It is our true Self. It existed in the eternal past and will continue to exist in the eternal future. Nothing can destroy it. The phenomenal world, which is the object of sense perception, may change from one form into another, but the Atman or Self will never change. It is absolutely unchangeable. "Weapons cannot pierce it, water cannot moisten it, fire cannot burn it, nor can the air dry it." It is indissoluble, immutable and immortal substance. It is not destroyed at the time of death. Death is the property of everything within the realm of time and space. All objects that have form are subject to death. Birth is followed by death. That which is born must die. Our body will die, because it had its birth and exists in space and time. But the Atman or spirit cannot die, because it was never born and is beyond space and time. If you try to think of the birth of your spirit, you will never be able to find an absolute beginning; therefore, Atman is beginningless and endless. Everything which can be perceived by our senses will change and pass away, while the Atman or spirit will remain forever.

Here it may be asked whether spirit is one or many? The same question may be asked of matter. Is matter one or many? We have seen that matter as objective substance is one, although it appears as many on account of its manifestations within space and time. Similarly, says Vedanta, there is one eternal Spirit or Subject of the universe, of which the individual spirits or egos are but so many manifestations. They are but parts of one stupendous whole or universal spirit or God. God is the eternal Subject or Knower of the world. He is the cosmic Ego, the sum-total of all individual spirits or egos and more. He is the one Infinite Being, the eternal ocean, which contains so many eddies or souls. The cosmic Ego or God is the first-born Lord of the universe. He is the first and highest manifestation of the Absolute Substance or Brahman. He is the material and the efficient cause of all phenomena. He is the projector of evolution. He differentiates subject from object, spirit or ego from matter or non-ego. In Him everything exists, through Him all beings live, and into Him they return in the end. He is more powerful than all the individual spirits together. We possess small powers; as our knowledge is limited so are our powers; but God is the one substance whose power is unlimited. He dwells everywhere. He forms the background of our individual spirit and possesses eternal knowledge. He is the Soul of our souls. We should meditate on Him and worship Him; then we shall understand the relation between spirit and matter.

"He is the one Eternal Being in the midst of all non-eternal forms and names. He is the one Source of intelligence in the midst of insentient matter. He makes that one substance appear as many and fulfills all desires dwelling within the hearts of all creatures. Whosoever realizes Him in his soul attains to eternal bliss even in this life."

"The infinite and eternal truth, Brahman, pervades the whole universe, the visible and invisible. If the visible be taken away, (if the perceptible phenomena be destroyed) that which will be left is the Infinite." May we realize the Infinite in this life; may we attain to that truth and enjoy peace forever.

"Peace, peace, peace to all living creatures."

Isha Upanishad.

KNOWLEDGE OF THE SELF.

The knowledge of God is not so commonly spoken of in India as the knowledge of the true Self. Self-knowledge reveals the knowledge of the real nature of the Absolute and of the Supreme Deity. Ordinarily we use the word "self" in the sense of ego, but the term "Self-knowledge" does not mean mere knowledge of the ego. The ego in us is the actor, thinker and perceiver. That which performs all the functions of the body and mind, is generally known as "I" or ego; but it is only the reflection of the Absolute Brahman, which is the source of all intelligence. The ego is the image of that divine spark within us which gives it vitality and makes it do all works mental and physical. So when we speak of Self-knowledge, we do not mean simply the knowledge of the lower animal self or ego, but also of the higher Self.

The higher Self is the same as the Absolute which lies at the foundation of the phenomenal universe. The Absolute Substance or Brahman is beyond space and time, consequently it is formless and unchangeable. When it manifests itself as an individualized, self-conscious entity, it is known as the ego. It also appears as the object of consciousness, then it is called matter; the Absolute Being, however, is neither matter nor is it the same as ego. It forms the background of our ego, therefore it is our true Self. When we have realized it, we have known God as well as the relation which the phenomenal universe bears to Him; and the best method of becoming conscious of this Absolute Being is through the realization of our true Self, or Atman, as it is called in Sanskrit.

Some people think that self-annihilation is the ideal of the Vedanta Philosophy, but it is not so. The true Self, according to Vedanta, can never be destroyed. If self-annihilation were the ideal, then the Self would be subject to change and destruction; it could not be the same as the Absolute Being. The Vedanta Philosophy, on the contrary, teaches that the true Self is absolutely indestructible and unchangeable. How is it then possible for anyone to think of its annihilation? Destruction of Self is just as impossible as the destruction of the Absolute; therefore self-annihilation cannot be the highest aim and ideal of life.

Self-knowledge alone helps us to realize the absolute Truth and to attain perfection. It is considered to be the highest wisdom. When Socrates asked the Delphian Oracle "What is the highest knowledge?" the answer came, "Know thy Self." By the word "self" here is meant not merely the ego, but the true Self. The same knowledge of the real Self has been glorified in India from the most ancient Vedic period. Vedanta, the rationalistic portion of the Vedas, describes this Self-knowledge as the highest ideal of life. If we wish to know God, we must first know our true Self; we must ask within ourselves who and what we are in reality, where we have come from, and what becomes of us after death? These questions are of vital importance. Ordinary people cannot solve such problems, their minds are too busy with the affairs of the phenomenal world. But an earnest seeker after Truth, who is discontented with the knowledge of material objects, wishes to go below the surface of phenomenal appearances and does not stop until the ultimate goal, the reality which underlies all phenomena, is discovered. His aim is to find the correct solution of these problems by knowing the true nature of his ego as well as of the universe. He may start with the objective world, but gradually, as he advances step by step and reaches farther and farther in his search after Truth, he comes back in the end to his own Self.

Because the true Self is the center of the universe. The phenomenal world, which consists of the objects of sense-perception, may be compared to a grand circle, the circumference of which lies in the gross material forms and the innermost center of which is Atman, the true Self.

The nature of this true Self, according to Vedanta is infinite. It is neither limited by time nor conditioned by space relations. The Scriptures describe God as the center of the universe, but Vedanta says that Self or Atman is also the center of the universe, and that the true Self is one with Divinity. The moment that we realize the Divine Self within us, we understand that the realm of the same Atman extends to the sun, moon, stars, and even to the most distant planets, the light from which takes hundreds and thousands of years to reach us. Wherever there is existence, whether on the physical or mental plane, there is also the manifestation of this Divine Self. That by which we know the existence of the external world, by which we are conscious of our bodies, senses and mental powers, is our true Self. It is not far from us, yet it is beyond the reach of mind and intellect. The Self is thus described in the fourth verse of the Isha Upanishad: "It (the Self) is beyond all vibration and motion. It is one, and swifter than mind. The senses never reached it, it transcended them all. Though standing still, it overtakes the mind and senses which are running fast. It is the source of all mental activities, sense-powers and the various forces of nature."

Modern science tells us that the whole world is the product of matter and material forces. Matter, again, as we have seen in the first chapter, is nothing but a certain state of motion or vibration of some substance, the true nature of which is unknown and unknowable. Every particle of the universe is in constant motion or vibration. That which we call heat or light, sound or taste, odor, touch or any object of sense-perception, is nothing but a state of vibration of the same unknown substance. Sir William Crookes says: "At thirty-two vibrations per second, is it shown that we have the first beginning of audible sound, and that sound ceases to be audible when it reaches to something less than thirty-three thousand vibrations in a second. The vibrations of heat and light rays are almost inconceivably more rapid. They are expressed in no fewer than fifteen figures, whilst the vibrations within a single second of the recently discovered radium are expressed in more than nine millions of millions of millions." The whole world consists in the vibration of atoms, or the most minute particles of material substance, but above and beyond all this vibration there exists the Absolute Reality, the true Self, which is the source of knowledge, intelligence and consciousness. It is through this Self that we know that there is such a thing as vibration.

Here the question rises: Who is it that

knows that the world is a mass of vibration? Does vibration know itself? It cannot. "Motion produces nothing but motion," this is one of the laws of nature which has been confirmed by modern scientists. Motion cannot produce knowledge. Knowledge is something which is not the effect of motion or vibration; but it is that which enlightens our minds and makes us see and understand that there is such a thing as motion or vibration. Therefore the Upanishad says: "That which does not vibrate is our true Self." Search within and see where is that which does not vibrate, but which is the Knower of all vibrations and actions.

"It goes faster than mind." We know that mind is the fastest thing in the world; thought travels faster than electricity, or any other current that exists on the physical plane. Sir William Crookes reasons that "the thought vibrations which issue from the brain may really have their beginning at a point where it becomes no longer possible to estimate the vibrations which are caused by the most subtle forces of physical nature." Furthermore, he adds: "If we can any way realize the concept of a force which is capable of creating thousands of trillions of vibrations in a second, and if we add to this idea that the velocity of these vibrations is equalled by their rapidity, we see easily enough that thought may put a girdle about the earth in an infinitesimal fraction of time."

We can exchange messages by wireless telegraphy between here and England or any other part of the world, but thought transference is quicker than wireless telegraphy. The mind of a person who is sitting here can go straight into the sun, or beyond the sun into the infinite space where the ordinary force of electricity will not reach perhaps—even there the mind can run in the shortest interval of time. Time exists in mind. What is time? Time means succession in thought. When one thought rises after another, the interval between them is what we call Time, so it is subject to mental activity. That which is swifter than mind is the true Self. Our real Self can go quicker than thought-current and even where mind cannot reach. It travels everywhere. Self or Atman forms the background of the mind, therefore the Self is quicker and faster than the activity of the mind. Mind can go nowhere without depending upon the Self, the Knower. It remains absolutely inactive when it is separated from the Self.

"The senses never reached it, it transcended them all." The senses cannot reveal it; sense-powers cannot express the true nature of the Self, because they are limited by time and space, while the Knower of time and space must necessarily be beyond the reach of the senses. When we see the sun, the very sight depends upon self-consciousness; that is, we must be conscious of the fact that we are seeing something, and that consciousness must depend upon our true Self. The sun will not be seen if our mind and eyes are separated and cut off from Self, the source of knowledge, intelligence and consciousness. Depending upon that source of consciousness and intelligence, our mind works, our senses perform their functions and the body moves. Therefore, the Isha Upanishad continues: "It (Self) moves and it moves not; it is far and likewise near. It is inside and also outside of all this." When the body moves, the source of intelligence, or our true Self, appears as moving, but in reality it does not move. Where will it go? It cannot go anywhere. When we move a jar from one place to another the space within the jar appears to be moving; but does the space move in reality? No. What is it then that moves? We do not know; the form appears to be moving, but the form again is limitation in space. It may be said, "If space does not move, then the form cannot move." It seems to be like a puzzle, when we try to answer it at every step we meet with insoluble problems.

The whole of life is a mystery. We endeavor to find some explanation by studying nature, but nature puts us into more confusion. Science does not help us; she takes us up to a certain point and there she leaves us without showing anything beyond, without telling us what to do and where to go. Such is the condition of our relative knowledge. When properly analysed, it appears to be a partial expression of the absolute knowledge, which is the real nature of the true Self. Relative knowledge, however, will not help us in solving the riddles of the universe. If we wish to know the ultimate Truth of the world we must go beyond nature and seek the explanation in the realm of the Absolute. Nature is called in Sanskrit *Mâyâ;* she deludes us, yet we are living in nature, and our body, senses and mind are parts of nature. The more we study nature, the more we are deluded; we do not come to any final solution. Scientists have arrived at certain conclusions, which are like conclusions in which nothing is concluded. Science tells us that the ultimate goal of everything is unknown and unknowable. Here Vedanta comes and advises its students to study not merely nature, but our Self or Atman; then all confusion will be removed and the Absolute Truth will be reached.

Nature makes us see that the Self moves when the body is in motion, but in reality the Self is immovable. Nature makes us feel that Self is very far from us, but it is the nearest thing that we have, nearer than this body and mind which we consider to be the nearest; our true Self, however, is in reality the nearest of all. "It dwells in everything as its soul or inner nature, yet it is outside of everything." How can that be? If it dwells inside how can it dwell outside? Space exists inside as well as outside. Take the space within this room, which is confined by its walls. This space appears as inside the room; but what are the walls, are they separate from space? No; they exist in and through space, they are nothing but space. The space of the walls limits the space that is inside the room; but does it limit in reality? No. It is outside also. Can we limit the infinite space? By no means. Similarly, if we try to limit our Self by our mind we fail, because mind is not large and strong enough to keep the Self out; sense-powers cannot limit it; physical forms can never divide it; because each one of these exists as related to the Self. The Self or Atman, when properly realized, appears as unlimited and infinite. We say that we are finite beings, but in reality we are not finite. There is only one Infinite Existence which expresses itself through finite forms. As finite forms, existing in space, cannot live outside of it, so all these various individuals live in and through that infinite space of Reality which is called the Absolute Self.

"He who realizes all beings in the Self, and the Self in all animate and inanimate objects of the universe, never hates anything or any being."* Hatred proceeds from imperfect relative knowledge, which makes us perceive objects as separate from one another. But when we see our true Self in others, how can we hate another without hating our own Self? It would be impossible for Self to hate Self. As it is impossible to hate our true Self, so it would be impossible to hate the Self of any being. This is one of the results of Self-knowledge, where Self-knowledge is there can remain no feeling of hatred. When hatred is gone, jealousy and all other selfish feelings, which we call wicked, disappear. What remains? The ordinary love, which stands in opposition to hatred, vanishes; but Divine love begins to reign in the heart of the Seer. True love means the expression of oneness. As love for body makes us feel one with the body, so love for the true Self makes us feel one with the true Self; and if we see that Self in others, we cannot help

* Isha Upanishad, verse 6.

loving them as we love our Self. Now we understand the meaning of "Love thy neighbor as thyself." It is not an extraordinary teaching. Vedanta has always taught this truth. People of the western world say that Christ was the only one who ever taught in this way, but they do not know that this is the very foundation of the ethics of Vedanta.

Love means the expression of oneness in thought, word and deed. "Where all beings have become one with the Self, what delusion, what sorrow can there be to him who has once realized this unity?"* Self-knowledge leads to realization of oneness with all beings. When all beings appear as parts of one universal Self, there is neither delusion, nor fear, nor sorrow, because there can exist no other thing outside of Self or Atman for which one can grieve or from which one can suffer. Sorrow and fear arise so long as there is the sense of duality or multiplicity.

---

* Isha Upanishad, verse 7.

If all objects of fear and sorrow become one with the all-pervading Divine Self, then fear and sorrow must vanish. But so long as we think of other beings which exist outside of our Self, we cannot avoid grief and suffering which arise on their account. In absolute oneness, however, there cannot remain fear, sorrow, suffering, separation or self-delusion. This is another result of Self-knowledge.

Some people may think that Vedanta teaches us to be selfish, but this is far from true. The self becomes dead; the lower self vanishes, and with its disappearance all selfishness is destroyed. The word "Self" must not be taken for lower self or selfishness. It stands for Atman, the higher Self, which is our Divine nature. There is no other expression in English by which we can convey the real meaning of Atman. We shall avoid confusion, therefore, if we use the Sanskrit word "Atman" to express our true Self. Then no one will mistake it for selfishness. "The Atman has pervaded all, effulgent, incorporeal, scatheless, untouched by brain or nerve centers, pure, sinless, a poet (Kâvi), wise, omnipresent, self-existent, he has disposed all things aright for eternity." * That Atman (Self), who is the center of the universe, is all-pervading. Wherever our mind goes, the Atman goes there. It is the source of the light of intelligence; it is pure, spotless, sinless. Here you will notice that Vedanta teaches that we are not born in sin and iniquity, but that our Atman or true Self is sinless. By this it does not encourage us to do sinful acts, but it tells us that the moment one acquires Self-knowledge, from that moment one ceases to do anything wicked. The Atman is in the body, but it has no body. It is formless, that is, beyond gross and subtle forms. There are forms which we cannot see except through the most powerful microscope, even such minutest forms do not affect the Self. It is abso-

---

* Isha Upanishad, verse 8.

lutely beyond all forms; but at the same time it can appear in any form, and all forms exist in it.

Atman is beyond all nervous activity, or the function of the brain. The materialists maintain that when brain and nerve centers vibrate, self-consciousness is produced. But Vedanta contradicts their statement by saying, "Beyond the reach of nerve centers and untouched by brain powers." It is not affected by the changes of the body; there may be variations in the color or form of the physical body, or the body may be diseased or have some part mutilated, but that disease or mutilation will not produce any change in the true Self or Atman. Therefore, Self-knowledge makes one free from nervousness and other physical ailments.

The word "Kâvi" means poet, and also means the seer of things. Self is described as the greatest poet of the universe; this is one of the most beautiful expressions and attributes that can be given to Divinity—

He is the poet, His poetry is the universe. He is also described as the greatest artist. His art we see in the sunrise and sunset. The sun, moon and stars are nothing but the paintings on infinite space by the hand of the Almighty artist.

True Self or Atman is above good and evil, beyond virtue and vice. Some people ask: How can it be above good and evil? Others say: It is only good. Good and evil, however, are two relative terms; evil exists in relation to good, and we cannot separate the one from the other. If we wish to take good, we shall have to take evil also. So with virtue and vice; one cannot exist without being related to the other. The Absolute Self is above all relativity; therefore, it is above good and evil, beyond virtue and vice. "There is no other seer than this Atman, no other knower." Who can be the knower of the universe? There is one eternal Knower who knows the existence of all objects, and the knower in us is only a part of that eternal

Knower or God. The vast majority of mankind do not know this great truth; the preachers do not teach it, because they themselves do not understand it. If God is the Knower of all, then the Knower in us is a part of God. Vedanta tells us to realize the individual knower first; then will the Knower of the universe be known.

The Atman or true Self is never the object of knowledge, but it is always the subject. The cosmic or universal Knower is the same as that which people worship as God. Thus by the light of Vedanta we can see God close to our souls; but in the Scriptures of special religions He is made remote, He is driven far out of our reach. Vedanta brings Him nearer than anything we possess. Although this Atman is all-pervading, yet it is beyond everything; it dwells in all things, still it is not the same as anything. It is never affected by phenomenal conditions. It transcends the changes of nature, yet it permeates nature. It is its own cause; in it cause and effect are identical. The Atman has no cause, yet it is the cause of all; and at the same time it is beyond the law of cause and effect. The Self has existed by itself from the beginningless past and will continue to exist throughout eternity; no one can see its beginning or its end, because beginning and end refer to time, and our search after them, being within the sphere of mental activity, is also subject to time. We may search for the beginning and end of the phenomenal universe, but as the Atman (Self) is above all thought and beyond time and space, it can have neither end nor beginning.

"It is all-knowing." All relative knowledge is only a partial expression of that wisdom which constitutes the nature of the Atman. Now we see that the attributes which people generally give to God, such as, He is omniscient, omnipotent, all-pervading, eternal, infinite, are also given by Vedanta to the Atman or true Self. True Self is the Soul of our souls. Self-knowledge reveals that the attributes of God are also the attributes of the Atman. "Those who do not realize this true Self, dwell in the darkness of ignorance and go through the misery and sufferings which exist in that darkness." They are always fearful and unhappy. They fear death and everything that threatens their earthly existence, and they make their life miserable by attaching themselves to a particular form of manifestation which they are afraid of losing. They love sense-enjoyments and worldly pleasures, they feel disappointed and discontented if they do not find these, and they consider that this earthly life has no other higher aim or ideal. The life of such persons is nothing but a continuous chain of fear and unhappiness. Those who are rich fear loss of fortune; those who have reputation and high position are afraid of losing them; while every man or woman suffers from the fear of disease and death. Do you suppose that these people will ever enjoy true happiness on this earth? No.

They alone are truly happy who have become absolutely free from fear. Perfect happiness comes and all fear is conquered when Self-knowledge is gained. For this reason each one of us ought to make constant efforts to acquire it in this life. The light of Self-knowledge dispels the darkness of ignorance and frees us from fear, sorrow, misery, birth and death, as also from bondage, imperfection and delusion, which proceed from ignorance.

This ignorance is likewise the mother of selfishness. It has the power to veil the Divine and absolute Atman and to make us identify our true Self with the material body. Thus when forced by the inscrutable power of ignorance (Avidyâ) we forget our real Self, think of ourselves as the sons or daughters of mortals, we become finite and subject to such limitations as are understood by the term "selfishness." Self-knowledge destroys ignorance and makes one absolutely unselfish. Blessed is he who lives in the sunshine of

Self-knowledge, having risen above the clouds of fear and selfishness which gather in the night of ignorance. What is this world? It is produced by ignorance and bound by fear. Knowledge of the Self destroys all worldliness, brings spiritual strength and makes one fearless, as God is fearless. Does He fear anything? How can He? The moment we realize that God dwells in us, how can we fear? How can we have fear of death when we know that death merely means a change from one body into another, and that our true Self or Atman is unchangeable? Those who do not possess Self-knowledge are miserable, and will be born again and again on this plane of ignorance until they have learned to realize their true Self.

Self-knowledge is the only source of happiness; it will lead to perfection and freedom. You may seek freedom, but how can you obtain it when you have become a slave of fear and earthly conditions? You are a part of Divinity. Feel it, realize it, and all these ties will drop away and you will be free. The attainment of this freedom through Self-knowledge will bring to you the realization of your oneness with Divinity. Then you will be able to say: "That light which I see in the sun is in me; and that which is in me is in the sun. I am the Lord of the body, senses and mind, and I am also the Lord of all phenomenal objects."

"I am the light of the universe, through me shine the sun, moon, stars and the lightening. I have realized my true Self. I have realized the true Self of the universe and therefore I am one with the Absolute."

"May my speech be established in my mind; may my mind be fixed in my speech. O Divine Word! Thou hast manifested Thyself in the form of wisdom. Do Thou spread Thy powers through my words. Do not deprive me of the truth. May I always dwell in the truth. My salutations to the fire of wisdom, to the seers of Truth and to the Devas (bright spirits).

"O Divine Word! be propitious to us; stay in our spiritual space and be happy. Like the Lord of Light (the sun) constantly purify our hearts and reveal to our eyes that which is auspicious for us. Do not leave us.

"Peace, Peace, Peace to all living creatures."

Kaushitaki Upanishad.

PRANA AND THE SELF.

Since the Vedic period, at least two thousand years before Christ, Self-knowledge has been in India not only the theme of sages and philosophers, but also the highest ideal of kings. Most of the early Hindu monarchs were, indeed, the great spiritual teachers of the country, although they did not belong to the Brâhmin caste. There is a prevailing idea that the Brâhmins were the only teachers of spiritual Truth in the beginning, while the duties of ruling and fighting were confined to the Kshatriya or warrior caste. Yet in the great epic Mahâbhârata it is told that some of the Brâhmins fought battles, commanded the army and showed remarkable powers, courage and ability, though they did not become rulers of the country. As in the Bhagavad Gitâ we read of Drona and Kripâchârya, who were Brâhmins by birth, yet who became noted generals, served on the battlefield, and were the teachers of the Kshatriyas in military science as it was known at that time. On the other hand, we find in the Upanishads and in the epics that the Kshatriyas were the first teachers of the Brâhmins in higher spiritual truths; Krishna, Râma, Buddha were all Kshatriyas. The Kshatriyas, being of the warrior caste, were bound by duty to protect the country, govern the nation, fight the enemies and establish the reign of peace, justice and righteousness among the people. They were entitled, however, not only to become soldiers, commanders of the army and to sit on the throne, but likewise to impart Self-knowledge to all sincere and earnest souls.

The Hindu rulers of those early days were not like the monarchs of to-day. They regarded life as something that had a meaning, and for them this early existence was not worth living until that meaning had been realized. Even in that early age these royal seekers after truth felt that those who perform the duties of their daily lives without knowing who they are and what they are in reality, are dwelling in absolute darkness. Therefore, after fulfilling their duties as Kshatriyas and rulers of the country, they still found time enough to devote themselves to the pursuit of Self-knowledge.

There was a great Hindu monarch of ancient India, by name Divodâsa, who lived in Benares. Benares was the Indian Athens of those days. It was the seat of education, and the center of religion, science and philosophy. From prehistoric ages it had been the cradle of oriental civilization and culture. Even at the time of Buddha, five hundred years before Christ, it was the stronghold of Hindu philosophy and religion; and Buddha could not have done anything if he had not been able to convince the learned scholars of Benares. Divodâsa, this famous and powerful ruler of Benares, had a son, who became renowned by defeating his fiercest enemies. It is said that he even conquered the Devas, the mythological gods or bright spirits. In the third chapter of the Kaushitaki Upanishad there is a story which describes how this young prince, Pratardana, by his wonderful courage and prowess conquered all the great ones on the human plane and then came to the abode of the ruler of the Devas.

According to Hindu mythology, Indra, the god of Thunder, became the ruler of the Devas through his righteous works and wisdom. Pratardana, the son of the mighty king Divodâsa, went to the abode of Indra, dwelling in his heaven, with a desire to conquer him. He told how he had destroyed his enemies and vanquished the Devas. Indra was somewhat dismayed at the sight of so great a hero, and did not know how he ought to receive him and what he should do to please him. So, after hearing the description of his powers and victories, Indra said to Pratardana: "I am well pleased with thee and wish to give thee a boon. Choose a boon and I will be happy to grant it to thee." The prince answered: "Do thou thyself choose that boon for me which thou deemest most beneficial for a man." He did not know for what to ask, but he knew that there was something which would be most helpful to all. Having in his mind the thought that people who are dwelling in ignorance and self-delusion and who do not understand the true nature of Being, ought to have something that would make their life worth living, he said: "Grant me that boon which thou thinkest best for a man." Indra replied: "That is not right; thou must choose thine own boon; no one who chooses, chooses for another." The prince insisted, saying: "The boon chosen by me is no boon for me." He would not choose because he did not know what would be most helpful to mankind, therefore he left it to Indra.

Then Indra said to him, "I am bound by my promise and I must be true to my words, so I must grant thee the highest boon that would be helpful and useful to all mankind."

"Know me only; that is the highest and most helpful for man. Know me, my true Self." He meant by this, not his powers, not his glory, but his real Self—that which is signified by all such expressions as "I, me, mine," and "thou, thee, thine." He who has known this true Self gains unbounded power. If he commits any wrong, that wrong does not affect him. The knower of Self is the greatest of all, he is greater than kings, greater than the mightiest emperor; he possesses all the virtues that are described in the Scriptures of the world and nothing can make him fall from the glory of Self-knowledge. Then Indra praised Self-knowledge by saying: "I have conquered all the demons, I have destroyed those demons who had three heads, one hundred heads. I have done many cruel deeds, but all these horrible acts could not affect me, because I possess the knowledge of the Supreme Self. Although I have performed many inhuman deeds, yet see my glory, strength, and power; not a single hair of my head has been injured by them. He who knows me thus is never harmed in his life by any sinful act, neither by theft nor by the murder of his father, mother or a wise Brâhmin. If he is about to commit a terrible sin, the expression of his face does not change." Thus Indra praised Self-knowledge. He did not mean that the knower of Self should ever perform all such sinful, cruel and inhuman deeds. He wanted to show that the power of Self-knowledge is greater than any other power that exists anywhere in the world; that it purifies the heart and soul of the worst sinner and washes off the most horrible sins that a human being can commit. The murder of either father, mother, or both, or the revered spiritual master, all these unpardonable sins cannot corrupt the Divine power of Self-knowledge, which purifies the souls of all who possess it.

After praising Self-knowledge, Indra said: "I am Prâna, know me as Prâna, life. Worship me as the conscious Self, the source of intelligence." Prâna is the Sanskrit word for life-force; life and intelligence are inseparable; wherever there is life, there is intelligence in some form or other. "Meditate on me as life and intelligence. Life is Prâna, Prâna is life; life is immortality and immortality is life." Here we must understand that life never dies. Life in itself is immortal and indestructible; it cannot change. We do not see life growing from less life. Life in the abstract is always the same whether or not it expresses itself outwardly. The expressions may vary, but the life-force is one and unchangeable. When we do not see the manifestation of life we say it is dead; but life-force does not die. Very few people can understand this. Where life is, death cannot exist. We may say a child is born, a child grows, but the life of the child is not subject to growth; if it were subject to birth and growth, it would be changeable, it would be mortal. That which we call life-force is free from birth, decay and death; all these changes take place in the forms through which the immortal life-force manifests itself. We speak of a child or a plant as growing, but from the very beginning the life-force is the same; the manifestations of some other powers with which life is attended, appear in different ways at various stages of the evolution or growth of the animal or vegetable organism.

"Prâna is life, life is immortality; as long as the Prâna dwells in the body, so long there is life. By Prâna one obtains immortality in the other world." If we know what true life is, and feel that we are one with life and inseparable from it, then we can realize that we are immortal, because life does not die, it does not proceed from non-life. If we try to trace the origin of life, going back in imagination as far as we can, we shall never be able to discover as its cause non-life or something dead. Life always proceeds from life. It has existed from the beginningless past, and we cannot think of its ever being subject to death or destruction; therefore it is eternal. But so long as life-force manifests itself through a body, the body appears as living; this is the secondary expression of true life-force. Here we do not think of the life-force or Prâna, but of the form which moves and does certain work. We say, "He lived so long," "His lifetime consisted of so many years, three or four score;" all these expressions, however, signify the secondary manifestation of Prâna. Life in its primary sense is immortal. When that Prâna or life-force expresses itself, then the organs are alive, the senses perform their functions, the mind thinks, and the intellect acts.

Again this Prâna or life-force is inseparable from intelligence; we cannot separate intelligence from the force which makes everything of the universe move. The Self has two powers, which express themselves as intelligence and as the activity of Prâna or life-force. Intelligence is that which is the source of consciousness; there is no English term by which we can express it. It is called in Sanskrit "Prajnâ." It cannot be translated as "knowledge," because knowledge means understanding, which is a function of the intellect; but Prajnâ refers to the source of all knowledge and consciousness.

Indra continued: "He who knows me as one with life (Prâna) and intelligence (Prajnâ), as immortal, indestructible and unchangeable, has life to its fullest extent on this earth, and after death resides in heaven and enjoys everlasting life." Here Indra used the word "Prâna" for life-force, but the young prince thought that he must have meant sense-powers, because Prâna is also used to signify the power of seeing, hearing, smelling tasting or touching, the power of speech, the powers of seizing, moving, excreting and generating, and that by which all the organs of the body perform their functions. Therefore, he said: "Some say that all the Prânas or sense-powers become one; for otherwise no one could see, hear, speak, and think at the same time. After having become one, each of the senses perceives separately." Thinking that by Prâna was signified the activities of the sense-organs, he wanted to know which of these was particularly meant by Indra. He maintained that although life or Prâna was one, still the sense-organs performed their functions separately in succession. Two sense-perceptions do not occur at the same moment, there must be a minute interval of time between them. For instance, when we see a sight and hear a sound apparently at the same time, proper analysis will show that the one sensation is followed by the other; we cannot have various perceptions simultaneously. According to the phychologists of ancient India, mind perceives the objects of sensation one at a time. When one sense-organ performs its function, others remain quiet; the interval may be infinitesimally small, we may not grasp it with ordinary attention, still they rise in succession leaving between them a very minute interval of time. So the young prince did not understand what particular sense-activity was referred to by Indra. After raising this question, he kept silence.

Indra replied: "It is true that all these senses perform their functions at certain intervals and that each one of them is great; but nevertheless there is another force which is higher than all the sense-powers. That force is preëminent among all other powers." It is not the power of seeing or hearing that makes us alive. Blind and deaf persons do not see and hear, but still they live. The power of speech does not manifest itself in a dumb man, yet he is alive. A man may live having lost the power of smelling, tasting or touching. Infants and idiots live though deprived of the thinking-power of the mind.

One may not have memory, still one will be called living. All this shows that that which makes one alive is not the same as the power of seeing, hearing, speaking, smelling, tasting, touching or thinking. Again, a man may lose his arms and may not be able to seize anything, still we do not call him dead. The loss of one's legs or other organs of work does not, as we see around us, destroy the life-force or the *Mukhya* (higher) Prâna. Therefore, the life-force is distinct from the power of perception or sense-activity. Yet at the same time these sense-organs will not perform their functions if they are separated from the life-force.

The life-force or *Mukhya* Prâna is something independent of the sense-powers, but the sense-powers are dependent upon life-giving Prâna. Where life-force is unmanifest, the sense-organs may remain perfect, but there will not be any expression of the sense-powers in the form of perception of sensation. The eye of a dead man may be perfect, the optic nerve may be in good condition, the brain cells may be in a normal state, but as the life-force is not working in that body, the sense-organs must remain dead, without performing their functions, without producing any sensation. Thus we can see that all the sense-organs remain active in the body because Prâna, the source of all activity, is there, and because the life-force governs and regulates all the senses. Therefore, in the Vedas it is said: "One should worship Prâna, the life-force, which keeps the universe alive." If you can understand what that life-force is you have understood the secret of the universe as well as that which keeps you alive.

All the scientists, anatomists, and evolutionists are trying to know the nature of that life-force, but have they succeeded? No. Some say it is a molecular attraction, others believe that it is the result of physico-chemical forces; but are they sure of what they say? What progress has science made in her attempt to find out the source of life-force?

Science has rejected the idea that the life-force is independent of the mechanical forces of nature; but she cannot tell us definitely the cause of vital energy. There have been debates and discussions on this subject among the scientists of different countries at all times; still the problem is unsolved. If we can understand the life-force of the universe we have understood the living God; because, says Vedanta, that life-force is inseparable from the Being who is worshiped as God.

What is God? He who keeps everything alive, and upon whom depend all other activities, sense-powers and the functions of the gross physical body. Indra said: "Prâna alone having animated this body makes it rise up. It alone is the conscious Self. What is Prâna is Prajnâ, self-consciousness; and what is self-consciousness is also Prâna. They both live in the body together and together they pass out of it." "That life is the same as our self-consciousness." Have you seen self-consciousness where there was no life? It is impossible. Wherever there is self-consciousness there must be life; self-consciousness and life are inseparable. You may say there is no self-consciousness in trees and plants; how do you know it is not there? Is it because they have no brain? They may not have the same self-consciousness as that of those who have brain, but they have nerves of their kind. How do you know a sensitive plant does not feel? All such dogmas of the theologians as that life is granted by the Creator to human beings alone, who would glorify His name, no longer appeal to us. Even the scientists of to-day, like Ernst Haeckel, are beginning to realize that every plant has its soul, that every cell has its own life, that every atom has its soul; and wherever there is soul there is also intelligence, the source of self-consciousness. It may be expressed imperfectly, it may be latent or waiting for proper manifestation; still wherever there is life there is some kind of intelligence; and wherever there is intelligence there must be life.

As we see in all living creatures, when life is gone, self-consciousness is also gone; so when life is in a state of abeyance, either in faintness or in swoon, when the life-force does not manifest itself in the form of organic functions or sense activities, self-consciousness at that time remains latent. Then Indra said: "When a man goes into the deep sleep state, where he sees no dream whatever, his mind is absolutely at rest, is enveloped, as it were, with a veil of ignorance." Sometimes when you wake up after dreamless sleep you feel as though you have come out of a realm of deep ignorance; in that state of sound sleep do you know what becomes of your sense activities,—the powers of seeing, hearing, smelling? They remain latent in Prâna, they go back and take refuge in that life-force. When the life-force remains inactive, then other powers also become inactive. In deep sleep we do not speak, see or smell anything. If there be the noise of a gun right near our ear we do not hear, neither does our mind think or imagine; all mental and physical powers remain potential, and come out as we wake up. The first awakening is visible in vital actions. In dreamless sleep (Sushupti), however, the life-force is not entirely separated from the central part of the body, because the subconscious activity of the Prâna is then manifested in the heart beat, in the circulation, digestion and in the respiratory process. If that force which causes the motion of the heart and lungs stops, there is absolute separation of the Prâna from the organs, then we do not wake. This is death. But in deep sleep we become one with Prâna, which absorbs all our conscious activities, and in the waking state they all return to their respective organs; the senses then begin to perceive and perform their functions.

Indra illustrates this by saying: "And when he awakes, then as from a blazing fire sparks shoot forth in all directions, so the sparks of the various sense-powers proceed each toward its place and come in contact with external objects." When a spark takes possession of the eye it illumines the object of sight, the form and color; another spark comes out and falls in the organ of hearing, it then illumines what we call sound. Similarly other sense-powers proceed from Prâna like sparks. The mind itself is another spark which performs various mental functions." But "when a person is going to die, being ill and falling into weakness and faintness, all the sense-powers go back to their source; then people say 'His mind has departed,' he cannot hear or see, speak or imagine. Then he becomes one with Prâna alone." As the Prâna leaves the body it takes with it all the sense-powers, which are dependent upon it. The dying man carries with him the powers of seeing, hearing, smelling, tasting, touching, seizing, moving, speaking, excreting, generating and the power of thinking as well as self-consciousness. All the vital forces and sub-conscious activities of the organs are also withdrawn when Prâna leaves the body. Along with these the objects, like color, sound, odor, etc., that are illumined by the senses, are also taken away. When the power of seeing, for example, is drawn away all colors and all forms, which can be perceived by the eye, go with it.

We shall see presently that the objects of the senses are inseparable from these sense-powers; when the latter are withdrawn, the objects are taken with them. If all the sounds and words which we utter be stopped, then the power of speech will remain latent, and with it will go all the names which can be illumined by the power of speech. For the same reason, when the power of smell is withdrawn, all the perception and sensation of odor accompany it; and all thoughts, percepts, concepts, memory, volition and ideas disappear when mind and intellect cease to be active. This absolute and complete oneness with Prâna happens at the time of death. Since Prâna and self-consciousness are inseparable, and since together they live in the body and together they go out of it, a man in this state is said to be dead.

All these organic powers which have been withdrawn with Prâna remain with him after death and he manifests them in another form. As in the state of waking after deep sleep mental and physical forces rise like sparks from a burning fire, so after the sleep of death all the latent powers come out from Prâna, manufacture other organs and perform their functions respectively. What is that force which manufactures the sense-organs? It is the Prâna or life-force, which contains in a potential form all the desires, impressions and tendencies of the previous existence.

When the activities of the senses, which reveal their objects, become latent, all sensations stop, and consequently ceases the relative existence of sense-objects. The Self is the center of intelligence and consciousness. It is clothed with the Prâna or life-force, a portion of which manifests itself subjectively as sense-powers, while other portions express themselves as objects of sensation. As the objects of perception cannot exist without being related to the perceiving sense-powers or subjects, similarly the subjects only exist as such so long as they are related to the objects.

Here we should remember the truths which we have already learned: that the sense-powers depend upon Prâna or life-force, that Prâna and self-consciousness are identical, and that objects are related to sensations because they cannot exist as independent of the powers of perception. There will be no color in relation to us if our power of sight be dead. For the same reason that which we call sound only exists in relation to the power of hearing. Similarly it can be shown that the external objects which we perceive are inseparable from our sensations of them, and these in turn depend upon our sense-powers. An object of perception may be compared to a piece of cloth. As a cloth which is made out of threads is identical with the thread (for what is a piece of cloth but threads woven together?) so an object of perception, being woven together of sensations and sense-powers is identical with them. The threads of sensations and sense-powers, again, are twisted out of the forces of Prâna. The whole universe, therefore, depends upon Prâna or self-consciousness; Self is the center of the universe as well as the center of each one of us. It is the foundation of life, inseparable from Prâna, and the producer of all sense-powers. Indeed, Self is the origin of the phenomenal universe.

Again it is said that this Prâna or self-consciousness is not many, but it is one. The life-force in you is the same as the life-force in me and in others. As life-force is one, so self-consciousness is one. The self-consciousness in you is also the same as it is in me and in all living creatures. It is one throughout the universe. We can only infer from external signs the nature of self-consciousness in other individuals and compare it with our own.

Self-consciousness lies at the root of all knowledge. For without self-consciousness speech does not make known any word; we do not perceive it. Without self-consciousness the ear cannot reveal any sound. When our self-consciousness is centered upon one particular object we do not see things which may lie in close contact with our eyes. For instance, when you are looking at something intently on the street, other objects may pass by in front of you, but you do not notice them though your eyes are there. So with sounds, when your mind is concentrated on one particular sound you do not hear other sounds; a person may be calling, but you do not hear it; so when your mind is concentrated on any particular thought or idea, you do not see, hear, smell or taste or have any other sensation. In short, without self-consciousness, no thoughts can rise in succession and nothing can be known. Therefore, it is said:

"That which is the real seer we must know; we must not try to know the speech or the words, we must know the speaker, the Self. Where is the speaker? Find it out. Who is the seer? Find it out. Let no man find out what speech is, but let him find out the speaker. Let no man find out what sight is, but let him find out the seer. Let no man find out what sound is, but let him know the hearer."

Scientists are trying to find out what sound is, but they do not care to know who is the hearer. Vedanta philosophers, on the contrary, go to the bottom of things; they do not care whether or not sound is the vibration of air. In order to become a sound any kind of vibration must be related to our power of hearing; if our power of hearing be withdrawn who will hear the sound? So what is the use of wasting our time in trying to know what sound is? First let us know the true nature of the sense-powers, then their source, and ultimately the Knower of all sense-objects. "Let no man try to find out tastes of food, let him know the knower of tastes. Let no man try to know what pleasure and pain are, let him know the knower of pleasure and pain. Let no man try to discover what joy or happiness is, let him know the knower of joy and happiness. Let no man try to know the thought, let him know the thinker. These objects of perception have reference to Prajnâ or self-consciousness, and the subjects or sense-powers have reference to objects. Objects have relation to subjects, subjects are related to objects; if there were no objects there would be no subjects, and *vice versa*. For on either side alone nothing can be achieved."

Self-consciousness is described by Indra as the center of the wheel of a chariot. This body is the chariot and the outer circumference of the wheel is made up of sense-objects, the spokes are the sense-powers, which reveal these objects, and the nave, on which the spokes are fixed, is the Prâna, the life-force.

Thus the objects are placed on the subjects (spokes) and the subjects on Prâna. The Prâna or life-force, which is inseparable from intelligence and self-consciousness, is imperishable, immortal, and blessed, that is the true Self. True Self is not increased by good acts, or decreased by evil deeds. The sins of the world do not corrupt or change the nature of this true Self. The true Self is neither virtuous nor sinful, but it is always Divine and perfect. Good and evil deeds affect the ego, the doer and actor, and bring in return the results which the ego reaps. We shall have to understand that all good and evil works are dependent upon self-consciousness and life-force or Prâna. The source of consciousness and intelligence is the guardian of the world, the producer of all phenomena of the universe, and that is "my true Self."

"And this Self-knowledge will help all humanity in the path of immortality and perfection, which leads to the abode of peace and happiness."

"MAY ALL THE FUNCTIONS OF OUR MINDS, WORKS OF OUR BODIES AND ACTIVITIES OF OUR SENSES PLEASE THE ALMIGHTY BRAHMAN, WHO IS DESCRIBED IN THE VEDANTA; MAY WE NOT FORGET HIM; MAY WE REALIZE HIS PRESENCE IN US; MAY WE NOT BE FORSAKEN BY HIM; MAY ALL DIVINE QUALITIES ADORN OUR SOULS AND BRING PEACE TO OUR MINDS.

"PEACE, PEACE, PEACE BE UNTO US ALL."

Chândogya Upanishad.

SEARCH AFTER THE SELF.

The ancient mythology of the Hindus, which resembles in many respects Greek mythology, describes how gods and demons took human forms and lived like human beings on this earth. Even in the earliest Upanishads we find accounts of such Devas (gods) and Asuras (demons) living together and fighting. It is told that the first-born Lord of the universe, Prajâpati, once said to the gods and demons: "Why are you fighting for power and supremacy? The knowledge of the Self alone brings peace to the knower. The Self or Atman is sinless, free from old age and death, sorrow and suffering, hunger and thirst. Its desires are true and never unfulfilled; and its thoughts are always true. This Self must be sought after by all. Whosoever realizes the Self obtains whatever he wishes, his desires are fulfilled, all powers come to him, and he becomes master of all worlds and of all the realms that exist on this earth as well as in the heavens."

The gods and demons, who were ambitious and unhappy, thought after hearing this that it was a very easy thing then to become lord of the world and master of everything. Here begins the story, given in the Chândogya Upanishad, one of the oldest and most authentic writings on Vedanta. It belongs to the Sâma-Veda, that portion of the Vedas which laid the foundation of the science of music in India. The scale of seven notes was first used in the hymns of the Sâma-Veda, which were put into music and chanted or sung during religious rites and sacrifices. The narrative tells that the gods and demons, being thus instructed by Prajâpati, the first-born Lord of all creatures, were awakened to a desire to attain Self-knowledge. They inquired among themselves how they could gain that knowledge, which would make them the most powerful of all beings, and they were determined to search for that Self (Atman), by knowing which all worlds and all desires are obtained.

Here we should understand that demons are not evil spirits, but they are like human beings, strongly attached to the pleasures of the sense-world. They know nothing of the higher ideals of life, they are materialistic in their views, and think that the body is all in all, and that everything is finished with the death of the body. They wish to rule over the whole universe, and their desires are never satiated; they always want more and more, and struggle constantly for power and strength. Human beings with such tendencies are described in the Vedas as Asuras or demons; while Devas, or gods, are those who are spiritual, righteous, self-sacrificing, who do not consider earthly enjoyments and worldly pleasures to be the final aim of life, and whose ideal is to gain spiritual strength and spiritual power and to realize the Absolute Truth.

These Devas and Asuras thought that if they could send their leaders to some seer of Truth, then from them they could gather Self-knowledge. So the gods and demons went to their respective leaders, Indra and Virochana, and requested them to go in search after Self-knowledge. Although they had all the pleasures and comforts of life and whatever human beings could wish for; although they possessed all psychic powers, property, wealth, luxury, and could get everything they desired, still they were not satisfied. They coveted more strength, more power, and when they heard from Prajâpati that there was something through which they could really become masters of the whole universe, they longed for it and were anxious to obtain it immediately.

Indra and Virochana, the rulers of the Devas and Asuras, set out separately to seek for a knower of Absolute Truth, who had realized the Self and who could impart his knowledge to others. They gave up their luxuries and pleasures, left their fine raiment and other possessions behind. With modesty and simplicity of manner, the two leaders, without communicating with each other, sought out the greatest of all the knowers of Self, and approached him with offerings in their hands in accordance with the custom of the country, for in India people do not visit a temple, king or spiritual teacher (Guru) empty-handed. So they took fuel, butter, fruit with them, and with due reverence offered these to him, regarding him as their spiritual master. Having received his permission, they became his pupils and lived the life of purity and righteousness like Brahmachârins, or students, for thirty-two years, always serving him and obeying his wishes. One day this holy master asked them why they had come to him and what they wanted. They replied: "We have heard from Prajâpati, the Lord of all creatures, that Self-knowledge can make one extremely happy and bring all powers and all objects of desire to the knower; that the real Self is free from sin and old age, unborn and deathless, unaffected by hunger and thirst; that its desires are ever fulfilled and its thoughts are true and perfect. This Self must be searched after and realized. We have come to thee, O Lord, to acquire Self-knowledge."

The great master, wishing to examine whether the understanding of these pupils was purified or not, did not instruct them in the highest Truth at the outset, but gave some suggestions, by which they could search out and discover the real Self that dwells within all. The best teacher is he who directs his students step by step in the path of realization and who makes them investigate the Truth by their own exertion. So the Divine master, who was Prajâpati himself in the form of a Guru, said to them: "The person that is seen in the eye is the real Self (Atman). He is free from sin, sorrow, suffering, and birth; immortal and fearless. By knowing him one can obtain all worlds and all desires." Hearing this, the minds of the pupils were confused. They could not understand what the master meant by the expression, "The person that is seen in the eye is the Atman, the true Self." They thought that he must mean the shadow that is seen in the pupil of the eye. When we look at a person's eye we see in it the image of a small figure, the reflection of ourself; the master, however, did not mean that. He referred to the real agent of seeing, the ruler of all the senses, who is seen through the senses by the pure-hearted Yogis alone. Thus misunderstanding the true meaning, the disciples asked: "Bhagavan, who is that which is seen in a mirror and perceived in the water? Is he the same person as the one who is seen in the eye?" The master, knowing that his pupils had not understood the true spirit, replied: "That real Self indeed is seen in all these." Know it and realize it. Furthermore, to test his pupils' power of understanding, he continued: "Go and look at yourselves in a bowl of water, and whatever you do not understand about the Self come and tell me." The obedient pupils went and looked in the water, and seeing the reflection of their bodies they came back and said: "Yes, sir, we have seen what you meant." The master asked: "Have you seen the Self or what?" The disciples answered: "We have seen ourselves altogether from head to foot, a perfect picture even to the hair and nails." In order to bring them out of this confusion the master said: "After having your hair and nails cut, put on your best garments, adorn yourselves with ornaments and look again in the bowl of water." Following his instructions, they cleaned themselves, and wearing beautiful dresses and rich ornaments, they looked at their own reflection in the water. The spiritual master then asked: "Do you see the Self?" They said: "Revered sir, we see ourselves just as we are now, clean, well-dressed and well-adorned." The master replied: "That is the Self, the immortal Atman, which is free from fear and sorrow." Know it and realize it. The disciples went away satisfied in their hearts. Prajâpati, seeing them at a distance, cried out: "You have departed without acquiring the knowledge of the true Self; whoever among you, whether gods or demons, will follow this doctrine will perish." But Indra and Virochana paid no heed to his words. They thought that they had realized the Self and went home feeling content.

Now Virochana, who had understood that the body was the Self, went to the Asuras, the demons, and preached the doctrine which he had learned. He taught them the most materialistic ideas, like those of the atheists and agnostics,—"The body is the Self; the body alone is to be worshipped and served. By glorifying the self and serving the body one becomes master of the worlds and obtains everything." The demons, following his instructions, became absolutely materialistic in their views and began to decorate and worship their gross physical forms.

Even in the present age many such demons are to be found in this world. Those who uphold atheistic, agnostic and selfish doctrines possess demoniac tendencies. They care for nothing but their own bodies and do not feel for others. They are not charitable, neither do they give alms to the poor. They have no faith in anything higher than their own material form. The demons of to-day offer no sacrifice to God. They decorate the body of the living or of the dead with flowers, perfumes, ornaments, and fine raiment, and vainly imagine that by thus worshipping the body they will conquer the worlds.

The lord of the Devas, Indra, however, had better sense than the ruler of the demons; he went home, but he hesitated to preach before the gods. Remembering what the Lord of all creatures had described, that "the Atman or Self must be free from hunger, thirst, birth, death and sorrow, that it is immortal and fearless," he said to himself: "This body cannot be the true Self, because it is subject to hunger and thirst, and is not free from any of these imperfections. How could the master have meant by true Self the shadow of this body, when the body is subject to birth, disease and death? I see no good result from this doctrine." Thus dissatisfied Indra determined to return to his master as a pupil with offerings in his hand. When he came again the master said to him: "You went away with Virochana satisfied in your mind that you had learned the truth and gained the knowledge of the Self; for what purpose have you returned?" Indra replied: "Bhagavan, how can the shadow of the body be the true Self when it goes through constant changes? If the body is well-decorated with flowers and beautiful costumes the Self (shadow) has a different appearance. If one loses ones eyes the shadow (the Self) will look as though blind, that Self (shadow) will be lame if the body is lame, crippled if the body is crippled, and will perish with the death of the body. Therefore, that changeable shadow cannot be the unchangeable Self. I do not see any good result from such a doctrine. Please explain my difficulty and make me understand the true Self." The master replied: "O, Indra, so it is indeed. I shall explain to you the true Self. Live with me as my disciple for another thirty-two years."

Indra lived with his master and served him for another thirty-two years. One day the master, being pleased with the purity, chastity and devotion of his pupil, instructed him thus: "That which enjoys all dreams during sleep is the true Self. It is the immortal and fearless Brahman (the Absolute)." Know it, realize it, and be conscious of it. Hearing this, Indra went home satisfied in his heart. But before speaking to the Devas he found another difficulty. He understood, The Self (Atman) which enjoys dreams is not the same as the shadow of the body, it is not affected by physical changes. It is true that this Self is not blind when the body is blind, or lame when the body is lame, nor is it injured if the body be injured; but how can the seer of dreams be immortal when it is subject to change and fear, and suffers pain in unpleasant dreams? Thus thinking, he said: "I do not see good in this doctrine; I must go again and ask my master concerning this perplexity." Indra went to Prajâpati, his spiritual teacher, the third time and questioned him thus: "How could that changeable seer of dreams be the true Self, which is unchangeable, immortal, free from sin, hunger, sorrow, suffering, birth, and death?" The master replied: "O, Indra, you are right. I will explain to you again, stay with me another thirty-two years."

At the end of that time the master said: "In sound sleep that which enjoys perfect rest and sees no dreams is the true Self or Atman, which is immortal." Indra thought, how can that be the immortal Self, which is not conscious of itself or of anything else? No knowledge or consciousness remains in this state. Everything is destroyed then. Did the master mean by Self the destruction of all thoughts, feelings, sensation, consciousness and knowledge? In deep sleep state we have neither feelings, nor dreams, nor sensations, nor consciousness of the body or of the external world. He could not understand how that state of annihilation could be the true Self, so he came back and asked the question: "Bhagavan, dost thou mean that true Self is the state of absolute annihilation of consciousness, knowledge, sensation and feelings?" The master answered: "No, that is not true Self." Here we should notice how the great spiritual master gradually directs the mind of the disciple from the gross physical body through the abstract to the Absolute. True Self is the Absolute beyond all comprehension. If we start from this state of dreamless sleep, rising above all feelings, thoughts and sensations, and if we can go still further we shall find our true Self. Now the master was extremely gratified to see his return and said: "Your understanding is profound; I will explain to you what true Self is. Live with me for another five years and no more."

At the end of the last five years the master imparted the highest knowledge to his faithful pupil: "This gross physical body cannot be the Self, it is subject to death, in fact, it is constantly attacked by death." The life of the body is nothing but a series of deaths or changes. Every particle of the body is continually changing, and if that change stops for a second the body will live no more. "By death this body is perpetually attacked; death is always working in the body." The word "body" here includes all the sense-organs. The organs of the senses are also subject to similar changes, consequently they are dying at every moment. "The body is the abode or instrument of the Self, which is immortal and without body." Through this instrument the Self or Atman comes in contact with the gross material world. If the true Self does not manufacture the body it cannot come in direct touch with the objects of the senses. The body, therefore, exists for the enjoyment of the Self; it is the medium with which the Self being identified, it thinks "I am the body" and experiences heat and cold, pleasure and pain. But the ruler of this body is the Self, while the body is its abode.

The real agent that perceives through the senses is the true Self within us. Sensations are produced by the contact of material objects with the sense-organs. The gross objects, having forms, cannot directly come in close contact with the Self unless it manifests itself through the physical form of the body. But formless is the true nature of the Self, who is the knower of this body, the enjoyer of sensations, the doer of all actions. "The Self," said the master, "has no particular form." It dwells within the body without having any special shape. We should bear in mind that our true Self is formless, although our body is with form; then we should understand that the changes of the body do not affect the Self. Since the Self is formless, how can it be the same as the shadow of the body? The lord of the demons, having his intellect covered with *Tamas*, the darkness of ignorance, and having an impure mind and an imperfect understanding, could not grasp the true meaning of the Self. The master waited for him to ask further questions, but as he went away satisfied in his heart that he had learned everything regarding the Self, Prajâpati was not anxious to force upon him his knowledge of the Absolute Self or Atman, which he was utterly incapable of receiving. Virochana, therefore, did not acquire the knowledge of the true Self, which is formless and immortal.

All the organs of the senses, all sensations, in fact everything connected with the body, is transitory; if we can realize this we can know that the immortal Self cannot be one with the body. This formless Self dwells in the body for a time, and after leaving it remains formless. "So long as the Self (Atman) lives in the body and is identified with it, it is not free from pleasure and pain, but he who knows the Self as separate from the physical abode, is untouched by pleasure and pain." It may be asked, How can the formless Atman manifest itself through the body which has a form? Wind has no form, steam has no particular form, electricity is formless, but still they appear through forms. When the wind blows, although it is formless, it comes in direct contact with objects with form, and shows its form and power by moving them; so, also, steam is without form, but think how it manifests its gigantic force through engines and locomotives. The atmosphere is filled with electricity, which is imperceptible to our eyes and senses, yet it takes various forms, such as lightning and thunder. We do not feel the presence of atmospheric electricity; it required a Marconi to make us realize the value and importance of this invisible current in the atmosphere. The forces of nature are always invisible and formless. No one has ever seen or touched a force *per se.* Its existence can only be inferred by seeing its manifestation through forms. As all the imperceptible forces can be perceived by the senses under certain conditions, so the Atman or true Self, although imperceptible by nature, manifests its power and intelligence through the form of the physical body. How can we know the power of thinking except by its manifestation as thoughts? In the same manner the existence of the powers of seeing and feeling is inferred from their expressions. If the sight remains unmanifested in a man we call him blind; and he is known as an idiot whose mental and intellectual powers have become latent; but when the expression of these powers begins we see their outward effects.

No one could have inferred what powers exist in the Atman if the true Self had not manifested through the body the powers of seeing, smelling, tasting, touching, moving, seizing, thinking, feeling, etc. They proceed from the Atman, the self-intelligent center within us. In the state of ignorance these faculties of the soul appear as produced by the body, which is mistaken for the Self; but when the light of Self-knowledge begins to shine the Atman reveals itself in its true nature as separate from the body and possessing all powers and intelligence. As an ignoramus cannot distinguish the wind clouds and electricity from etherial space, so a self-deluded soul cannot distinguish the true Self from the material organism. He who possesses Self-knowledge, realizes that the Atman is the Highest Being (Purusha). He is always happy, enjoying the play of life's sports under all conditions and never thinking of the material body, which is the mere abode of the intelligent Self.

The true Self, as we have already seen, possesses Prajnâ, intelligence, and Prâna, activity, these two will be found at the foundation of the phenomenal universe. When these are latent or potential there is no evolution. Vibrations of all kinds, cosmic or molecular, and all kinds of motion are but the expressions of the activity of Prâna. Intelligence is manifested by human beings, as also by lower animals, the difference being only in degree and not in kind of manifestation. Wherever intelligence, life-force or any kind of activity is to be found, there is the expression of the Self. No knowledge is possible without self-consciousness. First we must know ourselves before we can know anything. We may not know our real Self on account of imperfect understanding, still we possess some kind of self-consciousness. In Vedanta these two, intelligence and Prâna, are described as the ultimate generalizations of all phenomena of the universe; and they proceed from the Cosmic Self or Brahman, which is the source of all knowledge and of the activity of mind and senses.

Indra said: "The Self is the greatest Being in the universe." When properly understood we cannot separate this Atman or true Self from the universal or Cosmic Being, because there exists only one ocean of the absolute Being or substance which is called by various names, such as God, Brahman, Atman, Self. When that absolute Being expresses itself through our forms it becomes our true Self, the source of mental and physical activity, as well as of intelligence and consciousness. All desires are certain forms of mental activity; they could neither rise nor exist if the self-conscious entity were not at the foundation of all activities. He who has acquired Self-knowledge can live in the world performing all kinds of works, enjoying all pleasures, but at the same time without being affected or disturbed by any unpleasant condition of this world. The knowledge of Self protects the soul from being agitated by phenomenal changes. "As a horse, being yoked to a carriage makes it move, so this conscious Self, being attached to the chariot of the body, makes it perform its functions by the power of Prâna and intelligence." Or we may compare the body to an automobile, the propelling power of which proceeds from the true Self. If the Self be separated or disconnected from the organs of the senses the eyes will see no sight, the ears will hear no sound, the nose will smell no odor, the tongue will taste nothing, the hands and feet will perform no work. Indra continued: "The eye itself is only an instrument, the seer is behind the pupil of the eye. The real seer and knower of sight is the true Self. The nose is the instrument, but the knower of smell is the true Self. The tongue is the instrument of speech, but the knower of speech is the conscious Self; the ear is the instrument of hearing, but he who hears is the true Self. He who thinks is the true Self, and the mind is his spiritual eye. Through this spiritual or divine eye the Self or Atman sees all pleasures and rejoices." The mind, intellect, heart, are the instruments of the true Self, which is the knower of all mental activities.

"The Devas, who are in the highest heaven, worship and meditate upon this Self; therefore, all worlds belong to them and they have obtained the fulfilment of all desires. He who knows this Self and realizes it obtains all worlds and all desires." He who possesses Self-knowledge is the master of the world and lord of everything, like the gods of the highest heaven. In him all desires are fulfilled. He no longer desires anything of the world, nor does he seek happiness from outside. He possesses all powers; in short, he is omnipotent, omniscient and ever blissful. Thus the great master explained the mystery of the true Self; and the earnest, sincere and pure-hearted disciple realized it through his blessing. Indra served Prajâpati one hundred and one years, as it is said in the story. This shows that knowledge of the true Self cannot be easily acquired. Patience, perseverance, and earnest and sincere longing are the steps toward the attainment of Self-knowledge.

Indra became happy, and with gratitude in heart and salutations to his Divine master, he went home and gave the fruit of his hard labor to the Devas. All of them followed his directions, realized the Self and became masters of the worlds. Such is the power and greatness of Self-knowledge.

"May the Divine Self protect the teacher and the student. May he feed our souls with the nectar of eternal Truth. May he grant us spiritual strength. May our studies bring the realization of the Absolute!

"Peace, Peace, Peace be unto us and to all living creatures."

Kena Upanishad.

REALIZATION OF THE SELF.

A seeker after Self-knowledge, having performed all the duties of his life, discovered that the performance of duty could not bring peace to his mind. He had worshipped all the Devas or bright spirits, and had served the gods, but he had not received the knowledge of his real Self. Nor had he found satisfaction, although he had spent most of his time in devotion to the Supreme. Thus learning that happiness, peace and knowledge cannot be obtained from sense-objects or from earthly relations, and realizing the ephemeral character of the phenomenal world, he could no longer remain content with the pleasures of a worldly life, so he renounced all his attachment to earthly things.

He also gave up all studies, because he had

discovered that the reading of the Scriptures could not give Self-knowledge or absolute happiness; for books and Scriptures simply remind us of the higher truths, but they cannot bring the highest Truth within the reach of our soul. Those who think that spiritual realization will come from the study of the Scriptures and sacred books are mistaken. The Scriptures describe certain spiritual truths, such as the existence of God, Divine Love, salvation, but by squeezing the pages of the book no one can gain the realization of these truths any more than one can get a drop of water by squeezing the pages of the almanac, in which the annual rainfall is mentioned. Before we can comprehend the spirit of any Scriptural text we shall have to realize the truth described in it.

This seeker after Self-knowledge, therefore, abandoned all studies, and went to a spiritual teacher who had known the Self. He approached him like a humble pupil, longing to acquire Self-knowledge. He had no other desire; he did not care to go to heaven or to enjoy celestial pleasures; his sole aim and ideal in life was to know the true nature of the Self. Nothing else could please him or make him happy; his heart was longing for that nectar of wisdom which flows in the soul of a knower of the Atman. Though he had come to understand that the physical body was not all in all, that the mind, the director of the senses, was not the unchangeable Reality, but was subject to constant change, yet his thirst for knowledge was unquenched. Now he was eager to search after that unchangeable and absolute Truth, which is the Soul of our souls and the Ruler of all. Having bowed his head with deep reverence at the feet of the great spiritual teacher, the pupil asked: "Revered Sir, who is it that governs the mind, and by what power is the mind directed to perform its functions? What force guides the Prâna and the sense-powers? Why is it that we are so active, what is the cause of our activity? Who is this speaker of words? Who is the seer of sights? Who is the hearer of sounds? What power controls the organs of sight, hearing, and the other senses?"

With this inquiry begins the Kena Upanishad, which had been handed down through memory for generations before the art of writing was known in India. It shows how old and sublime are the teachings of Vedanta. Think of the antiquity and the deep meaning of these questions! We know that our mind is constantly active; new thoughts and ideas are rising and going down. Mind wanders from here to there; sometimes it is in England, or in India, sometimes it runs to the sun, moon, stars or other planets; hence the seeker after Self-knowledge asked: "Who is the director of this constant activity of the mind?" The master answered: "That which is the hearer of hearing, the thinker of thoughts, the speaker of words, the mover of all activities of the sense-organs, the seer of sights." Let us understand the meaning of "That which is the hearer of hearing." First of all we must inquire, What is meant by hearing? Hearing signifies that power by which we perceive the existence of what we call sound, or in other words, that organic activity which illumines the vibration of sound; so the hearer of hearing refers to the illuminator of the power of hearing, without which no sound can be heard. The spirit of the master's reply was, The director of the mind is that which illuminates the powers of hearing, seeing, thinking, and of speech, as well as the knower of all the activities of our sense-organs.

The power of seeing, again, means that organic function by which the object of sight is illuminated or made known to us. The organ of sight, however, has not the power to produce consciousness or intelligence. The power of seeing exists so long as there is Self-consciousness behind it. The organs of vision, as the eye, the retina, the optic nerve, the brain cells, together with all their activities, do not produce the consciousness of color or the object of vision. In a dead person all these organs may be in a perfect condition, but the perception of sight or the sensation of color will not be felt by the body. The body itself has not the power to see or perceive any external object. Thus by analyzing our perceptions we can understand that the activities of the sense-organs are unconscious by nature. The conscious Self which illumines the organic functions is the seer of sights, the hearer of sounds, and the knower of all sensations. It is also the thinker of thoughts within us. That intelligent Self, which is the source of consciousness and knowledge, must be known as the director of the mind and senses. When we have realized the cause of self-consciousness, we have understood the power which directs the mind.

According to Vedanta, mind is "finer matter in vibration." The vibration of the mind substance produces perceptions and sensations, and reveals things which cannot be revealed by vibrations of grosser matter. The functions of the mind are nothing but the vibrations of the finer particles of the etherial substance called in Sanskrit *Sattwa*. But the vibration of this substance does not produce intelligence or consciousness. It is insentient by nature. The mind substance appears as intelligent when it is in close contact with the conscious Self or Atman, just as a piece of iron, having absorbed the heat of a furnace, appears as red-hot and is able to burn. The conscious Self may be compared to a magnet which attracts the iron of the mind substance. When a piece of iron, being attracted by a magnet, moves, that motion is not natural with the iron, but is caused by its proximity and close contact with the magnet. As the very presence of the magnet produces activity in the iron, so the very presence of the Self (Atman) creates the activity of the mind substance; but the Self is not confined within the limits of the mind substance, because the true Self is beyond all relations of space and time.

The master continued: "Knowing this Self, the wise, being freed from this world, become immortal." Those who have known that source of intelligence, the true Self, attain to immortality, but those who have not known it remain attached to the material body and senses, and are therefore subject to birth and death. This is one of the results of Self-knowledge,—knowing our true Self we become immortal. Although the true nature of the soul, according to Vedanta, is immortal, and immortality is our birthright, still we do not attain it until we have become conscious of our immortal Self. So long as we think that we are mortal we have fear of death. When the consciousness of the immortal Self is gained all fear vanishes. Fear of death rises from ignorance, which makes us forget our immortal nature and identify ourselves with the material body, which is subject to death. Thus, becoming one with the mortal body, we begin to fear death and suffer from anxiety and misery. How can we expect to be free from fear of death when we have identified our Self with the body, which will surely die? This fear, however, ceases to trouble him who has realized that the body is like a shell, a house, or a receptacle of the soul, which is deathless by nature. The soul manufactures the physical body in order to fulfill certain desires and purposes of life. He who has known this truth has risen above all fear. Therefore, it is said: "Those who have obtained the knowledge of the real Self are called the wise, and after the death of the body they transcend the realm of birth and death. This is the greatest object to be achieved in this world of relativity.

We have come here to fulfill a certain purpose. At present we may think that the highest purpose of earthly life is to gain material prosperity, success in business, fulfilment of ambition and sense desires; but the time is sure to come when we shall realize that all these are momentary, that the real purpose of life is much higher and more permanent. It is very difficult to understand the true purpose of life. Few people in this world have found a perfect standard by which they can measure correctly whether or not they have fulfilled that purpose. Each one of us will have to find out what is the highest ideal of life. It is the attainment of Self-knowledge.

Self-knowledge brings to the soul absolute freedom. It is by Self-knowledge that we can obtain everything we desire. In this world there is nothing higher than the knowledge of the true Self. The knowledge which we now possess is imperfect, it is only a partial expression of the all-knowing nature of the Divine Self. That imperfection is due to the limitations or imperfect conditions of the Buddhi or intellect which reflects the Divine wisdom. But when the limitations are removed and the intellect is purified true and perfect wisdom begins to shine within. If the mirror be covered with mud, it will not have the power to reflect the light of the sun; so when the mirror of the intellect or Buddhi is covered with the mud of worldliness, it does not reflect the light of wisdom which emanates from Atman the Divine Sun. In order to learn this truth and the method by which our intellect and heart may be purified we need the help of a Guru or spiritual master. Knowledge is one, not many. The same knowledge which we now possess will be the highest knowledge when it will reveal our immortal Self. Therefore, the wise men who know the true Self, attain to immortality even during this lifetime.

The pupil desired to see that Self, which is the director of the mind and the seer of the sight, and by knowing which one becomes immortal. The master said: "The power of seeing cannot reveal the Self." The disciple thought: "If the eye cannot reveal the Self its nature may be described." To this the teacher replied: "Words fail to describe it; the mind cannot reach it. We cannot know it by mind, intellect or understanding how can anyone teach it?" The Self is the thinker of thoughts. Mind can only think when directed by the Self who is beyond all thoughts. The very act of thinking presupposes self-consciousness, and all thoughts are only possible through self-consciousness; therefore, that which is above and beyond all thoughts cannot be revealed by the mind or intellect. When the mind cannot think of it how is it possible for the eye to see the true Self? The power of sight can reveal that which is in relation to our eyesight. The true Self can never be brought within the reach of sense-perceptions. The master continued: "It is far from the known and also it is above the unknown. Thus we have heard from the ancient sages who taught us this." From ancient times the great seers of Truth have declared that the real Self is neither known nor knowable, and yet it is neither unknown nor unknowable. Ordinarily we say, "We know a thing," "the knowledge of this book," etc. In this sense the Atman can never be known or made an object of knowledge.

Let us understand this clearly. When we speak of knowing a thing we mean relative knowledge by intellect; and we convey the same idea when we say "we do not know a thing." Again, intellect can reveal those things which are related to the senses or are subject to sense-perception. It is more or less dependent upon sense-powers; consequently its sphere is very limited, for the senses can reach only within a small circle. For instance, we hear sound through our ears. The sound is audible within a certain degree of vibration; if the vibration of air be above or below that scale we cannot hear; although there may be a tremendous noise, still our ears are deaf to it. The same may be said of the eye; the range of sight is equally narrow. Now we can see how very limited that intellect must be which depends upon these powers of perception. Therefore, that intellectual knowledge, which is related to sense-perceptions, is secondary knowledge; it cannot reveal the Self; hence it is said that the "Self is far from the known." Furthermore, when we say "we do not know this thing" we mean that we are conscious of our ignorance, we have the knowledge of the fact that we do not understand it or know it by intellect. This ignorance is nothing but the lack of the intellectual apprehension of the thing, which we have called secondary knowledge. It is, however, revealed to us by another knowledge which does not depend upon intellect or upon sense-perception. That apperception by which we know that we do not know this thing proceeds from the Self. Therefore, the Self is neither known nor unknown, but beyond relative knowledge and ignorance. "We have heard it from our great masters which passed away before us." Although this Upanishad of the Sâma Veda is very old, still the teacher here refers to the authority of other seers of Truth who preceded him and from whom Self-knowledge had been handed down through generations.

The master said: "That which cannot be expressed by speech, but which is the speaker and director of speech, that alone know as the highest Self (the Brahman); not that which people worship here." Every attribute that we give to God is not His attribute in reality. We call Him good, but He is not merely good; strictly speaking, He is beyond good and evil. We project our idea of good, mentally separate it from evil, and increasing its dimension, attribute it to the Infinite Being and call Him good. At the same time we forget that that which is good demands something better, and that better again requires something which is best. This shows how foolish we are when we seem to be contented after calling Him good. God is in reality beyond our conception of good, which is relative and limited. In this manner it can be shown that every attribute which we can think of, nay, every word which we can utter is finite in its meaning and idea. Yet if we go a little deeper we shall find that no thought can exist and no word can be uttered unless there be the self-conscious thinker and speaker behind. This self-consciousness is caused by the light of intelligence which proceeds from the Self. Therefore, the Self is the absolute Truth inexpressible by speech. It is the illuminator of speech, but it can never be illumined by words.

Is Self (Atman) the same thing which is worshipped by all the great devotees and worshippers of God? Is it some Personal God dwelling outside of us and directing our minds and senses by will and command? Is Self the same Being who is called by different names, as Father in heaven, or Allah, whom we worship with prayers and offerings? Is the Atman the same as an angel or bright spirit? What is it? Reading the mental question of his pupil the master said: "Not that which people worship here." The worshipper of a Personal God with a name and form is not the worshipper of the absolute Truth, because he worships the phenomenal God. Name and form being both phenomenal, our conception of the Divinity with a name and form is phenomenal and anthropomorphic, or in other words, we create an ideal God by projecting our ideas, give Him attributes according to our conception and then worship Him by offering Him our prayers. Prayers are nothing but words; we send these words to the Personal God in order to obtain certain results, but He, to whom we pray with words, is not the director of speech. That Self which is in us and makes us speak and pray is different from that which we worship with prayers. The Personal God with a form and a name is not the highest. This may seem strange to us, but we cannot deny it. God with a name and form, who can be described by words and thought of by our minds, is not the Absolute. There is a saying, "When God is known He is no longer God, He is our imagination." The Absolute

Divinity is different from that which is worshipped.

Again, that which can be thought of by the mind is not the Absolute Truth or Brahman. Therefore, the master said: "That which cannot be cognized by the mind but by which all mental functions are cognized, know that to be your true Self (Brahman), but not that which people worship." "That which cannot be perceived by the eye, but by which the eyes are made to see, know that to be the Self (the Absolute Brahman), not that which people worship." "That which cannot be heard by the ear, but by which the ear is made capable of hearing a sound, know that to be the Self (the Absolute Brahman), not that which people worship." "That which cannot be perceived by the power of smell, but by which the organ of smell perceives odor, know that to be the Self (the Absolute Brahman) not that which people worship." These verses show that the true Self, who is the director of the mind and senses, is not the same as the Personal God whom people worship, but it is one with Brahman, the absolute Truth.

Having heard this, the seeker after Self-knowledge went into meditation and searched for the illuminator or director of the mind, that which is beyond the reach of our thoughts, words and sense-powers. He spent some time in Samâdhi or the superconscious state, and realizing the Self he returned to the ordinary plane of consciousness and said: "I have known and realized the absolute Truth, I have known the Self." The master replied: "If you think that you know the Self, then you know very little of it." If you believe that you have known the Absolute Brahman perfectly, you have known very little of the Truth which dwells in you as well as in the universe. Truth is one. When you begin to think that you have known the Truth, you are using your secondary knowledge of the intellect, which cannot reveal the Absolute. If you imagine that you have known the Self or Brahman, who is the director of the mind, you have comprehended very little of it. If you think that you have realized it as dwelling in your body, you have not understood its absolute nature. If you believe that you have cognized it as dwelling outside your body, still you have not realized the Truth. If you have known the Self as God, the Creator of the universe, you have apprehended very little of it.

Here the question rises, "Why is it that we have known very little of the Self if we have known it as dwelling in our body?" Because that something which is the director of the mind does not dwell in one place; it is beyond the space relation. Therefore, when we have known it as dwelling in a particular place and not anywhere else, we have not realized the Truth. Again, if we have perceived it as dwelling outside of us and not in us, then also we have not known that this Being is all-pervading and beyond the relation of time and space; but we have known only that much of the Infinite which is limited by time and space and conditioned by their relations.

Then the disciple sat in meditation once more, and his soul, rising above the plane of thoughts, entered into the superconscious state. Having remained there for some time he came back to the planc of sense-consciousness and declared: "I do not think I know the Self well, nor do I know that I do not know it at all. The Self is neither to be known nor is it the same as that which is absolutely unknown; he who has known this truth has realized it (the Absolute Brahman)." What he meant by this was that Self-knowledge is beyond relative knowledge and ignorance. Whatcver wc know by the understanding is only possible through the light of intelligence which proceeds from the true Self; there is no other knower of the Self, who is the illuminator of mind and thoughts. The Self is in reality the eternal knower, there is nothing in the universe that can know the true Self, yet it is the source of all the true knowledge that we possess. It is always the subject of knowledge or consciousness, but never its object. Furthermore, the disciple said: "He who thinks that the Self (Brahman) can never become an object of knowledge thinks rightly; but he who thinks 'I have known it,' has not realized its true nature. The Self (Brahman) is not known by those who think it is known; but it is realized by those who think it is not known."

This seems an enigma; what does it mean? If we analyze our perceptions what do we find? When we see a color, we find that the sensation of color is produced by light which is a certain kind of vibration of the ether. A ray of light coming in contact with the retinæ causes some kind of molecular change in them; this being carried by the optic nerves into the brain cells creates certain molecular vibration in those cells. It requires a conscious ego to translate this vibration into a sensation, which we perceive and call color. If the conscious ego be not there, then these vibrations may be carried to the brain centers where they may produce other changes, but still we shall not see the color. For instance, when we are looking at a color, if our mind be suddenly distracted or concentrated on some other object, the color may remain before our eyes, yet we do not see it. Although the vibration of light has been carried to the brain centers, the molecular changes have been formed and all the physiological conditions are fulfilled, still we have no sensation of color, because there is no one to translate the molecular vibrations of the brain cells into the sensation of color. The ego who translates them is concentrated on something else. But when the changes are translated by the ego into sensations, then we perceive it. Now let us go a little deeper. Behind this intellectual perception there is the self-consciousness of the ego. If the ego be unconscious, if there be no sense of "I," then these vibrations will come through the senses and pass away without producing any sensation in the mind. Again, if the mind be separated from the source of apperception and intelligence, then the sensations will remain in the subconscious mind without affecting the conscious ego. This source of consciousness in us is the knower. It is our true Self.

We know that we are sitting here; when we walk, we know that we are walking; when we perform an act, we know that we are performing it; this knower of all acts and thoughts is the director. Is that knowledge different from our true Self? No, it is inseparable from our Self; our true Self is like a sea of intelligence. Some people say that knowledge proceeds from the Self, or in other words, that from which this knowledge proceeds is the Self. This would imply that the Self is separate from knowledge and would raise the question, "What is then the nature of the true Self?" According to monistic Vedanta the true nature of the Self or Atman or Brahman is absolute knowledge or absolute intelligence which never changes.

The functions of the intellect and mind are changeable, but Self-knowledge is unchangeable. Suppose you have a feeling; when it rises, you feel it and know that there is that feeling; when it subsides and another takes its place, then also you know that the new feeling is there. The knowledge by which you cognize each feeling cannot be known by any other knowledge, for there is only one knowledge in the universe; consequently the knower of that knowledge cannot be known by any other knowledge. That by which you know the existence of a feeling or a sensation cannot be revealed by intellect, understanding or any other faculty. Upon it depends intellectual understanding. Whenever we perceive any object through the senses, that knowledge is a partial expression of the Self or absolute knowledge, which directs the mind and senses to perform their functions.

The nature of the Self is all-knowing; its knowledge does not depend upon the relation between the knower and the object of knowledge, but it remains unchanged even when all the objects of knowledge have ceased to exist. The all-knowing Self may be compared to the self-effulgent sun. As the nature of the sun is to illumine himself as well as other objects, so the light of the Self illumines its own nature as also the phenomenal world. The sun himself can illumine everything as well as his own form, we do not need a candle or a torch to see him; therefore, we call him self-effulgent. Self-effulgence does not need any other light to illumine its nature. For the same reason the Atman is said to be the self-effulgent sun of knowledge. That knowledge by which we perceive all sensations and feelings, organic functions, intellection, understanding and other activities of the mind as well as external objects, the sun, moon, stars, is the light of the self-effulgent Atman or Self, which is the source of intelligence and consciousness.

This self-effulgent Atman is the knower and director of the mind and senses. The mind and senses will not perform any function if they are separated from the self-effulgent light of knowledge. Mind, as we have already seen, is "finer matter in vibration." Vedanta does not teach that mind is the same as the Self or spirit. There is no intelligence in the vibration of the mind substance. It is not the source of consciousness. All the activities of the mind may stop, still we shall remain conscious of our Self. In the state of Samâdhi there may not be any feeling, like fear, anger, or any other modification of the mind substance, such as volition, desire, emotion, will, determination, cognition, or understanding, but still one does not lose self-consciousness or become absolutely unconscious in that state. This will prove that pure consciousness or pure intelligence is separate from and independent of mental functions.

All these functions and sensations can be stopped by entering into superconsciousness; in short, one can cut off all connection with the body and mind and still continue to be conscious on the higher plane. It will be difficult for those who have not realized Samâdhi to grasp this truth. Intellectual knowledge will not reveal the Self; we must learn the method of going beyond intellect and rising above the realm of thoughts if we wish to realize the Absolute Self or Atman. Intellectual apprehension being relative and imperfect, cannot transcend the limits of phenomena and cannot reach the sphere of the Absolute. Therefore, it is said, "He who thinks he knows the Self knows it not."

Self-knowledge precedes even the conception of God. If the thought about God, which is in our mind, be separated from self-consciousness it instantly vanishes and becomes non-existent. We know God because there is knowledge in us, because the light of the Self reveals the existence of God. If this be so, we ask: Which is higher, the Personal God or the Self? The Self is higher, because it illumines the existence of God. This source of all knowledge, which is the absolute Truth, is higher than a Personal God, since the Personal God, who can be described by words and thought of by the mind, becomes subject to the mind and speech, consequently to the Self or Atman, which is the director of the mind and speech, and that which is subject to a thing must be lower or less than that which governs it. So when we try to know our true Self, we do not attempt to know it as we know the existence of a book or a tree, because that kind of knowledge will never reveal it. We must not try to see any form, because there is no form in the Self. We must not make the objects of the senses, like sound, color, odor, touch, the starting point of our search after Self, for these are on the relative plane, while the Self is the Absolute Being.

Thus we can understand the difference between the relative plane and the absolute. So long as we are on the relative plane, we cannot reach the Absolute, because the absolute knowledge, by which we know the existence of things which are related to one another, is beyond all relations and infinite. All relative phenomena exist in and through the Absolute, but the Absolute Atman is independent and self-existent. If we were unintelligent beings and did not possess Self-knowledge, then these sensations and perceptions would have no relation to us. The pure knowledge of the Absolute Self may be compared to the thread which goes through the pearls of percepts, ideas and thoughts that rise in our minds, and strings them together into one harmonious whole, forming a garland of our daily experiences. This pure knowledge must not be confounded with the relative knowledge which is finite and related to ignorance, or non-knowledge. The Self, being the knower of ignorance, is higher and greater and its light of absolute knowledge is that by which we realize that we know this or do not know that.

In Vedanta it is said: "The Self is the knower of that which sees, hears, thinks or perceives. It is the knower of the body, senses, mind, intellect, and heart with which we identify our Self." Through this identification, when the Self appears as the ego, then we say that we are the hearer, seer, perceiver and thinker; but the ego sees, hears, thinks and perceives, being dependent upon the pure knowledge of the Self. In fact the ego cannot exist without Self-knowledge. Self-knowledge and existence are one and the same. We know that we are here; if for a moment we forget that we are in this place or if we become unconscious of our surroundings, we shall remain non-existent, as it were, in relation to our environments. Thus although we may try to separate our Self-knowledge from our existence, we can never do it; for pure knowledge or consciousness and existence are inseparable. When we have realized Self-knowledge, we have understood our existence and discovered that the director of the mind is all-knowledge and all-existence. We say the sun exists; why? Because we are conscious of him; when we are not conscious of him, as in trance, he does not exist in relation to us. Self-consciousness, therefore, is the standard of all relative knowledge and relative existence. Herein lies the beginning and end of the existence of all objects which we can think of or perceive. The moment that we are unconscious of our body and everything of this world, they will cease to exist in relation to us. We all experience this truth during our sound sleep, when our conscious connection with the body being cut off, it ceases to exist and consequently we do not claim anything of the material world as belonging to us. But as our consciousness returns to the body, instantly the body together with everything related to it appears as belonging to us. Therefore, it is said that knowledge and existence are one.

Vedanta gives these two attributes to the Absolute Self, who is the director of the mind. The first is absolute existence, in Sanskrit "Sat"; and the second is absolute knowledge or intelligence, "Chit" in Sanskrit. These two, as we have already seen, are one and inseparable. A third attribute, however, is also given in Vedanta. It is called in Sanskrit "Ananda," meaning pure happiness or blissfulness. Where absolute knowledge and absolute existence prevail, there is also absolute happiness or blissfulness. It is different from changeable pleasure or relative happiness. Unchangeable blissfulness again is always attended with absolute peace. Wherever there is true happiness, there must be absolute peace, and the mind will not seek anything else, but will enjoy it and will try to possess it and never be separated from it. The ordinary pleasures, which we mistake for true happiness, may be agreeable for the time being, but in the next moment we dislike them and try to get away from them. Think how transitory are the pleasures that can be derived through the senses, they last only for a short time and in the reaction make us miserable. True happiness, however, is unchangeable. It brings no reaction and is everlasting. In the state of absolute existence and pure knowledge alone can be found absolute peace and true happiness. Such is the realm of our true Self, which is above all relativity and beyond all conditions of this earth. This indivisible Sat-chit-ananda, absolute Existence-intelligence-bliss, the disciple realized in Samâdhi as the director of the mind and the source of all the phenomena of the universe.

He then said: "Whosoever realizes that which manifests within us as the conscious Self, attains to immortality." Death means a change of the body. The body may die, the mind may die, the senses may die, but pure knowledge can never die. When we know that something is dying and if we do not identify ourselves with it, but become conscious of our absolute Self, then we are sure to attain to immortality. If we once grasp the idea that we are the Absolute Being, how can we ever be changed by death into a non-being?

As being cannot come out of non-being, so it cannot go back to non-being. Pure existence can never become non-existence; this is the proof of immortality. The Absolute Self or Atman is the immortal Being. It is also Brahman, the beginning and the end of the universe. The same eternal Being is worshipped as God under various names and forms. He is the Being who dwells in us and is inseparable from our true Self. The Absolute Being is not many but one. If there were many Absolute Beings they would be limited by each other and consequently not absolute. That one Absolute Being alone is immortal and deathless, and by knowing it we become immortal. No Divine Incarnation can give us immortality, if we do not possess it already. The Christian belief that immortality can be obtained only through the grace of Jesus the Christ, is not founded upon the knowledge of the immortal nature of our true Self. The students of Vedanta are not deluded by such statements; they try first to know the real

Self and then they realize that immortality is their birthright.

Since the true Self is the source of all strength, the disciple said: "We gain strength and immortality by Self-knowledge." Real strength comes to us when we have known that which is changeless and immortal. The spiritual strength which is gained through Self-knowledge is greater than material, physical, mental, and moral strength together. All other powers, except spiritual strength, are subject to change and death. Few people understand the meaning of "spiritual strength." By the word "spirit" is not meant a disembodied spirit, but the Absolute Spirit or Self or Atman or Brahman. Spirit is that Self which is the source of absolute intelligence and which is the Absolute Being. Knowing it, one attains to spiritual strength, which is higher than physical or psychic strength. With physical strength a man can kill a tiger or destroy thousands of mortals, but it will not protect him from death. He may possess material strength, but it will not save his life at the last moment. He may gain psychic power and do wonderful things, but that will not stop the changes of body and mind. Spiritual strength, however, which Self-knowledge brings, makes one free from birth and death. He who has gained physical and psychic powers will remain subject to birth and death, but if he can know that immortal Being, he becomes a master of the universe. The gigantic forces of nature serve and obey the command of him who has acquired Self-knowledge. "If a man know this Self here, he has gained the Truth." In this world of imperfection he who has known the Self has realized the Absolute Truth and has fulfilled the highest purpose of life. He has attained absolute freedom, perfect peace and true happiness in this life. But "if he does not know this here, for him there is great suffering." He who does not realize the Self comes back to this earth again and again, and, remaining in ignorance, seeks sense-pleasures and suffers great sorrow and misery. He does not escape the law of Karma and reincarnation.

"The wise ones, who have realized the all-pervading absolute Self (Brahman) in all animate and inanimate objects, become immortal after departing from this world." The knower of the Absolute and Immortal Self becomes one with it and remains as the immortal and perfect Spirit forever and ever.

"That which is the Infinite is Bliss. In the finite there is no bliss. Infinity alone is bliss. This Infinity is to be realized.

"The Self (Atman) is the Infinite. Self is below, above, behind, before, right and left; Self is all this.

"He who sees, perceives, understands, and loves the Self, delights in the Self, revels in the Self, rejoices in the Self, becomes the lord and master in all the worlds."

Chândogya Upanishad.

IMMORTALITY AND THE SELF.

In the Brihadâranayaka Upanishad of the Yajur Veda we read that there lived in ancient India a great sage, Yâjnyavalkya by name. He was a seer of Truth and lived a pure, virtuous, and righteous life. He had a devoted wife, whose name was Maitreyi; he performed all the duties of the householder as also of a good citizen, and lived in peace, doing good to others. As the result of all these good and unselfish works his heart was purified and his eyes were open to spiritual Truth. He understood the transitoriness and impermanent nature of the phenomenal world, and realizing that the life of a householder was only a grade in the process of evolution, he desired to enter into a higher state and make further progress. He had discovered the foolishness of people who lead a worldly life and constantly try to fulfill their earthly desires; therefore, he made up his mind to live a life of seclusion, and devote the rest of his days to the pursuit of eternal Truth. He wished to take refuge in the absolute Reality of the universe by retiring into the forest where he would not be disturbed by the world. Constant meditation upon the true Self had become the aim of this great seer.

One day he came to his wife and said: "Beloved Maitreyi, verily I wish to retire into the forest, leaving with thee my wealth, property and whatever belongs to me. Enjoy these and grant me thy permission." On hearing this, Maitreyi felt extremely unhappy, but being spiritually-minded, she asked this question: "Bhagavan, please tell me, if I possess the whole earth with all the wealth it contains shall I gain immortality by it?" She was not like the wives of to-day, who are greedy for wealth and possessions and who are delighted to acquire a little inheritance; she was not ambitious for material property like a woman of the world, but she understood that immortality was the highest of all treasures. Being guided by this ideal, she questioned: "Shall I be immortal by possessing all the riches and property which thou art going to give me?" "No," replied the sage, "if thou possessest the property and wealth of the world thou wilt live like the rich who enjoy, in whatever manner they desire, the luxuries, comforts and pleasures of earthly existence. There is no hope of gaining immortality by wealth. None can ever become immortal by means of riches or material possessions." Then the wife said: "What shall I do with that thing which cannot bring me immortality? If thou hast anything by which I shall become immortal please give me that. I do not care for thy wealth." Her husband, the great sage, replied, "Thou art truly my beloved; thou hast spoken well, it is worthy of thee. If thou desirest, I will tell thee of that by which one can attain immortality. Come and listen attentively to what I will say."

He first explained the true nature of the object of love. People love their parents, children, husbands, wives, property, wealth, and all other things that they possess, but they do not know what they love in reality. The real object of love is not a material thing, but that which lies behind the material form. O beloved, verily I say unto thee: "A wife loves her husband not for the husband's sake, but it is for the sake of the Atman, the Self, who is within, that the husband is loved." The wife does not love the dead particles of matter which make up the body of her husband, but she loves the soul, the Atman, which lies behind his form. "The husband loves his wife not for the wife's sake, but it is for the sake of the Atman, the Self, who is within, that the wife is loved." The physical body of the wife is not dear to her husband, but her soul, the Atman, is dear to him. The husband will not touch the dead body of his wife, he will not love it when her soul has departed from it. People love their children, not for the children's sake, not for the material form of their children, but it is for the sake of the Atman, the Self, that the children are loved." When a mother loves her child, do you think that she loves the matter that makes up the face or the body of the child? No, it is the Self that, dwelling behind the material particles, gives the child its form and attracts the soul of the mother. Love cannot exist on the material plane; it is the attraction between two souls on the spiritual plane of the Self. When people love their friends and relatives, that attraction of the souls lies at the bottom of the expression of their true love.

"Verily wealth is not dear, O beloved, that thou mayst love wealth, but that thou mayst love Atman, the Self, therefore wealth is dear." The center of love is the Atman or Self. When we love wealth or property, our attraction is toward the omnipresent Self, whether we are conscious of it or not. We love animals, like dogs, horses, birds, not because of their material forms, but for the Atman, the Self, which resides within them. In this manner Yâjnyavalkya showed that wherever there is true love there is the expression of the real Self or Atman. "None, O beloved, loves an animal for the animal's sake, but for the sake of the soul of the animal." The dead material body of an animal cannot inspire love in our souls. "People love the priests (Brâhmins), the warriors (Kshatriyas), the celestial worlds (Lokas), the bright spirits (Devas), the Scriptures (Vedas), and all other animate and inanimate objects, not for the sake of those objects, but it is for the sake of the Self (Atman) that each of these is loved."

When a person loves another for the sake of his own lower self or ego, it is an extremely selfish love; but when that love is directed toward the Self or Atman which dwells in another person it is no longer selfish; it gradually leads to Divine Love. In everything abides the one Self or unchangeable spirit which attracts our souls. We do not know the nature of that Self or Atman toward which all love, whether selfish or unselfish, is directed, and from which all love proceeds, whether for wealth, property, or material objects. A miser loves riches, but he knows perfectly well that riches mean nothing but a medium of exchange, that they only bring certain pleasures and comforts of the body. He is attached to his lower self, and for that reason he loves wealth which enriches his ego. The lower self of such a man is the center of attraction, and everything that brings happiness to it is very dear to him. "Therefore, O Maitreyi, the Self (Atman) is to be realized, to be heard, to be thought of, to be meditated upon. O beloved! When the Self has been heard, thought of, meditated upon and realized, then all is known." Thou shouldst know the true nature of that Self, which is the center of all attraction, from which all love proceeds and toward which it is directed. It should be heard and meditated upon constantly; when the mind is concentrated upon it, its true nature will be revealed. By the realization of the true Self, through constant hearing, concentration and meditation, Self-knowledge and immortality will be gained.

Yâjnyavalkya continued thus: If a person loves and cares for another only for his material body and possessions, the lover is abandoned by the loved one. If we care not for the Self of another but love the dead matter, believing there is no soul in the person, do you think that person will be pleased? No, that person will desert us instantly. If we love a priest (Brâhmin) knowing that there is no Self in him, we shall be abandoned by him. He will immediately leave our company. If we go to a king, thinking that there is no Self in him, that he is only a mass of dead matter, we shall not be loved by him, but on the contrary we shall surely be forsaken by him. He will drive us out if he realizes that we love him not for himself but for his material possessions. "For the same reason, he who knows there is no Self in the heavens, in the gods (Devas), in the Scriptures (Vedas), in animate and inanimate objects, shall be abandoned by each one of these." If we think of a departed friend, believing there is no soul in him, we shall surely be deserted by him. If we love God, knowing Him as a mass of insentient matter, without loving His spiritual, Divine and immortal Self or Atman, He will never come to us; we shall be forsaken by Him. Thus we can understand that whosoever knows anything elsewhere than in the true Self or Atman is and should be abandoned by everything, because everything exists as related to the Self. "The Self is all and all is the Self." Whatever we see, perceive or think of, is inseparably connected with the Self (Atman); it is one with the Self, and is in reality nothing but the Self.

Here it may be asked: How is it possible for us to realize that everything is the Self? To explain this Yâjnyavalkya gives the following illustrations: "Now as the sound of a drum, when beaten with a stick, can be differentiated from other sounds by referring it to the drum or to the drumstick, which is the source of the sound, and not by any other means, so the existence of a particular object can be differentiated by referring it to the Self (Atman) which is the source of all knowledge and consciousness and without which nothing can be known." "As the sound of a conch-shell or a pipe when blown cannot be differentiated without referring it to the shell or to the pipe, as the sounds of a lute when played can be known only by referring them to the lute; as these particular sounds are but various manifestations of one common sound, so the one common Self or Atman, which is the Reality of the universe, appears through the varieties of names and forms which we perceive with our senses." "As from the one source of fire, when kindled with damp fuel, gradually emanate clouds of smoke and flame which did not exist there before, so verily, O beloved, from the one great Being, the Self (Brahman), the common source of knowledge and intelligence has been spontaneously breathed forth all the knowledge that we possess, such as the four Vedas (Scriptures), the various branches of science and philosophy, and everything that exists in this world as well as in celestial realms."

Ordinarily we ascribe scientific knowledge to particular individuals, but in reality every kind of knowledge that we find in different people,—scientists, Yogis, and philosophers, —has proceeded from that one source, the Self. As from one fire proceed smoke, sparks and flames, so from this one Infinite Self have come out all the sciences, philosophies and spiritual truths described in the different Scriptures of the world, as also the truths of art and history. The knowledge which we possess and make use of in our daily life is the expression of that absolute knowledge which is eternal, one, indestructible and unchangeable, and which brings immortality to the knower, who realizes the Self.

At the beginning of the cosmic evolution all phenomena as well as all knowledge evolved from this one Infinite Self or Brahman. Just as a human being naturally breathes out the air that has entered his lungs, so the latent energy of the Brahman spontaneously breathed out knowledge and all phenomena which had potentially existed in it before the evolution of the universe. Again, at the time of dissolution these return to that Infinite Being and remain latent as the energy of the Brahman in the same manner as rivers, streamlets, brooks and all waters that exist anywhere will eventually flow into one ocean. The ocean of the Infinite Brahman is the final goal as well as the source of all knowledge and phenomena of the world. "As the source of all taste is in the tongue, of all touch in the skin, of all smells in the nose, of all colors in the eye, of all sounds in the ear, of all percepts in the mind, of all knowledge in the intelligence, so the source of all intelligence is the Self or Atman or Brahman."

Thus Yâjnyavalkya explained to his wife how the Infinite Self is the Beginning and end, the Alpha and Omega of everything. At the time of evolution everything comes out of it and during involution or dissolution everything goes back to the same source of all. The Infinite Self, Atman or Brahman, is one mass of intelligence without a second; there is no duality or multiplicity in this one substance. "As a lump of salt has neither outside nor inside, but it is a mass of taste, so indeed the Absolute Self has neither outside nor inside, but it is altogether a mass of intelligence, unlimited, beginningless and endless."

This infinite Being appears in two aspects, the universal, which is called Brahman, and the individual, which is called the Self or

Atman. As the source of individual consciousness, it manifests itself in various forms when it is connected with our body and senses; but when it leaves this material body, the senses cease to perceive their objects and the elements return to their causal states from which they arose. After death one cannot perceive the objects of senses. "O beloved! Verily I say unto thee, although the Self is a mass of intelligence having departed from the body, it possesses no particular consciousness of a mortal." The expression of intelligence on the sense-plane stops after death.

On hearing this, Maitreyi replied: "O wise lord! Thou hast bewildered me by thy statement, 'This mass of intelligence possesses no particular consciousness after death.' How can it be?" Yâjnyavalkya answered: "O beloved! I do not say anything bewildering; imperishable is the nature of the Self (Atman)." For thy enlightenment I will explain it to thee. "The Self is deathless and immortal by nature. So long as there is the duality of the perceiver and the object of perception, so long one sees, perceives the other, one smells the other, one tastes, touches, thinks, and knows the other." The individual Self perceives sense-objects so long as it remains on the plane of duality or relativity. The perception of sight is possible only when the seer is related to an object of vision. If we are not related to that which we call odor how can we smell it? The ego can hear a sound or taste a savor by coming in direct relation with those objects of sensation. In this manner it can be shown that all perception and sensation require the relation between the subject and object; but when we go into deep sleep we do not see, hear, taste, smell or perceive anything. These objects exist on the sense-plane, but when we are above and beyond it and have gone to that plane where there is neither sight nor odor nor smell nor taste, how can we see, hear or perceive anything? All individual souls, who are in the state of dreamless sleep, become equal in their realization; we cannot distinguish the soul of a man from that of a woman so long as he or she is in sound sleep; then it is impossible to differentiate them. Similarly, in the state of Samâdhi or superconsciousness, where there is neither duality nor multiplicity, but the infinite ocean of intelligence, what can be seen or heard or smelled or tasted? Where there is neither relativity nor any object of perception, how can one touch or know or think of anything? "How can one know that by which one knows all this?" Is there any power of knowledge, by which we can know the Self, who is the knower of all? No; because the true Self alone is the Knower of the universe.

If we seek to know the Self within us what will be the best method? By right discrimination and analysis we can differentiate the knower from the object of knowledge. In this process of discrimination we must mentally reject everything outside of the knower by saying "Not this, not this." Thus when all objects of knowledge, including all sensations, perceptions, thoughts, feelings and other mental and intellectual functions are removed by right discrimination, the all-knowing Self is realized in Samâdhi. The Self or knower cannot be comprehended by intellect; it is incomprehensible. The Self cannot perish; it is immortal. The Self cannot be destroyed by anything; it is unchangeable. The Self is unattached; it is not touched by any object. The Self is unfettered; it is free. It does not suffer; it is beyond all suffering. It does not fail, it is always the same. "How, O beloved, can such a Knower be known and by whom? Thus far, O Maitreyi, the true nature of the Self can be described; and beyond this is the realization in Samâdhi (superconsciousness) which brings the attainment of immortality. He who has realized the Self, has become immortal. The knowledge of that Self, which is the source of all love, the source of intelligence, existence and all that is blissful, makes one attain to immortality." Thus saying, Yâjnyavalkya, the great seer of Truth, retired into the forest, devoted his time to meditating upon that eternal. Self, and, ultimately realizing his true nature in Samâdhi, he gained immortal life.

Self-knowledge being the goal of life, by that alone we can understand the universe, how it has come into existence, why it stands, and where it will go after dissolution. By knowing our true Self we can know what will become of all phenomena at the time of general involution, and if we wish to become immortal, we must know this Self or Atman; there is no other way to immortality.

"I know this great Atman, radiant like the self-effulgent sun and beyond the darkness of ignorance. By knowing Him alone one crosses the ocean of death; there is no other way; there is no other way."

Great Saviors of the World

(Vol. I.)

A NEW BOOK

BY

SWAMI ABHEDANANDA

Cloth, $1.00 net. Postage, 6 cents. Portrait of each Savior.

CONTENTS.

I. Great Saviors of the World (Introductory.)

II. Krishna and His Teachings.

III. Zoroaster and His Teachings.

IV. Lao-Tze and His Teachings.

"These studies are scholarly and comprehensive reviews of historic fact. They are also broad and open interpretations of moral and spiritual forces. The author's attitude is reverent toward all. His mind is free. His speech is peculiarly impressive. Surely, it speaks well for the world that its people can look without bitterness and jealousy upon the fact that God has sent, and will send, many Saviors into the world. This is a good study, fitted to open the heart and liberalize mind."—*Washington Star*. June 29, 1912.

"A valuable contribution to metaphysics."—*Portland Oregonian*. June 23, 1912.

"The work is taken up somewhat in chronological order. . . . The teachings of the thinkers who form the subject of the lectures are faithfully reported. The author holds no special brief for any of those remarkable men but endeavors to state precisely what their ideas were. The style of the author is interesting as well as perfectly lucid."—*Buffalo News*, April 21, 1912.

Swami Abhedananda emphasizes the similarities in the teaching of these great men. His aim is "to show that the fundamental teachings of the founders of the great religions of the world have had the same spiritual keynote and that the stories connected with their lives and miraculous deeds are similar to those of Jesus Christ."—*St. Paul Pioneer Press*, August 4, 1912.

Press Notices.—*Continued.*

"He (author) attempts to explain their ideas accurately and pays much attention to the legends of the east relative to the origin of the great leaders in sacred affairs."—*Des Moines Capital*, June 5, 1912.

"It sets forth in picturesque language the principal events in the lives of his heroes and gives a good concise idea of their teachings." —*The Indianapolis Star*, May 26, 1912.

"Swami Abhedananda's discourses point to the essential harmony of religions . . . and offer an unusual opportunity to study from conemporaneous expressions the companion viewpoints of faith and pure culture."—*New York World*, May 25, 1912.

"The life and teachings of three great Sages, of whom the Western world knows far too little, is treated in a wonderfully clear and attractive manner. . . . Their illumined efforts in lifting up a new ensign for the people of their respective countries are described by an Oriental Scholar, who is perfectly fitted for the task, and has familiarized himself with the available records of their almost superhuman labors. Each of these great souls is made to live again in the respective chapters of this engrossing work, very interesting side lights are thrown on alleged inaccuracies, many abscure points are made plain, and the underlying principles they set out to teach are conveyed in simple, but scholarly style."—*The Column*, June, 1912.

"Swami's book will do infinitely more good at the present time in the west than any book he could have written upon the different schools of Vedanta."—*Vedanta Universal Messenger*, Dec., 1912.

"It breathes the spirit of deep vision and profound learning and one sees that the Swami is actuated by the spirit of his Master, Sri Ramakrishna, that Synthesis of the Religious Consciousness. . . . The quotations from learned authors, bearing relation to the historical features of the Avatâras with which the book is replete, shows how diligently the Swami has prepared himself for his arduous task. He has left nothing unsaid.—*Awakened India*, Nov., 1912.

"This collection of lectures by the well-known Vedantist constitutes the first of a series of three volumes dealing with the same subject. As the author indicates in his preface, the word "Saviour" is used by him in the broad sense, and not as denoting "a Saviour who saves from eternal damnation." The present volume deals with the lives and teachings of Krishna, Zoroaster, and Lao-Tze, viewed in the unifying light of the Vedanta. The many admirers of Swâmi Abhedânanda's works will welcome this addition to the list, whilst those who have not yet had the pleasure of becoming acquainted with the grandeur of the teachings of this religio-philosophy, through the light of which "the Unity of the Godhead under variety of names and forms" may be perceived, will assuredly read the book not only with interest, but come from its perusal with the conviction that the Swâmi possesses the happy gift of bringing to light in an interesting and attractive manner the harmony existing between the leading world-religions."—*Occult Review*, July, 1912, London, England.

IN THE PRESS

GREAT SAVIORS OF THE WORLD

Vols. II. and III.

Human Affection and Divine Love

BY

SWAMI ABHEDANANDA

Flexible cloth. Price, 50 cents. Postage, 3 cents.

A suitable gift-book full of inspiring thoughts. It describes the evolution of Love in its various stages—animal, human, and divine; and shows that love is not an emotional sentiment as commonly understood but an attribute of our REAL SELF.

"Beautifully expressed sentences, on the idealism of love, reflected from India."—*Portland Oregonian*, June 23, 1912.

"Never under any circumstances is divine love an evil thing, but is everlasting in its beneficent blessings. In this little book the author contrasts the enduring beauty of the divine love with that of human affections which if misdirected in its selfishness results in murder, robbery and other crimes. His book is divided into two parts and the latter includes numerous quotations to prove his argument."—*Des Moisnes Capital*, June 5, 1912.

"It is written simply and the mysticism in it is somewhat akin to the mysticism of Mæterlinck, Emerson and of Thomas á Kempis—different as they all are."—*St. Paul Pioneer Press*, Aug. 4, 1912.

"A tiny book but containing a volume of profound thought wisdom and beauty. It was Drummond who wrote that the greatest thing in the world was "Love," and since then love has somehow had a greater significance and more exalted place in the world than it ever occupied before. But even Drummond did not put it on the high plane or give it such exquisite meaning as this writer has. He casts away the material and shows that the love that exalts, the love that worketh only good reaches through the material to the divine."—*Oregon Journal*, April 28, 1912.

Press Notices.—*Continued.*

"Human affection has ever been manifested in attachment to some object, and the enlightened passages in this practical little volume show the same tendency on the animal plane by means of a very fine comparison. The nature and expression of Divine Love is also very skillfully analysed, and a nice distinction drawn, between it and the human quality. The author feelingly portrays an ideal behind both, which might well be adopted by the individual, and typified in his relation to others in daily life, with invaluable results to all. The words of the Swami on "that Divine Love that knows no fear," but realizes everything comes from God are uttered in a dècisive style that will appeal to an army of souls, who to-day feel the truth of such a principle. Those will be greatly helped by the plain and highly intelligent explanation of a great truth, in which the vividness of Oriental expression is reproduced in Western terms by a master of both languages. This especially applies to the closing chapter where aptly chosen illustrations so dear to the oriental mind elucidate the two characteristics of ecstatic love, the three states of consciousness and their correspondence to the five sheaths of the soul, beyond which is the True Self, the Absolute. An elevating manual quite in keeping with the Author's previous best work."—*The Column*, June, 1912.

"It is thoroughly sound and happily written book, a fine introduction to Bhakti Marga. It is profitable reading to every person while to the more philosophically inclined it affords valuable instruction."—*The Brahmavadin, Madras India*, Dec., 1912.

"Carefully does the Swami draw the distinction, showing how human love attains its climax in directing itself to God."—*Awakened India*, Nov., 1912.

"This is a book presenting somewhat of the old Indian philosophy, which is noble and pure. It is in no sense a departure from Western thought, as one might be led to suppose. It is well written and free from metaphysical speculations."—*Brooklyn Eagle*, June 24, 1912.

Unity and Harmony

A New Lecture by

SWAMI ABHEDANANDA

Price, 15 cents. Postage, 2 cents.

Divine Heritage of Man.

BY SWAMI ABHEDANANDA

12mo, 215 pages. Portrait of author, frontispiece.
Cloth, $1.25. Postage, 8 cents.

CONTENTS. I. Existence of God. II. Attributes of God. III. Has God any Form? IV. Fatherhood and Motherhood of God. V. Relation of Soul to God. VI. What is an Incarnation of God? VII. Son of God. VIII. Divine Principle in Man.

"The Swâmi Abhedânanda's writings are also companionable and readable. . . . The Philosophy of India, being the bringing together of the best thoughts and reasonings of the best men for the thousands of preceding years, had under consideration the self-same problems that are to-day vexing the souls of our philosophers. The Swâmi's book is therefore not so radical a departure from accepted thought as might at first be imagined. . . . It is not meat for babes, but rather will it give new lines of thought to the brightest intellects."—*Transcript*, Boston, Aug. 1903.

"His method of dealing with these fundamental questions is peculiarly free both from dogmatic assertion and from pure metaphysical speculation."—*Inter-Ocean*, Chicago, Aug. 1903.

"He bases his arguments, not on theological hypotheses, but on scientific facts."—*Cleveland Plain Dealer*, Aug. 1903.

"It is written in a plain and logical style, and cannot fail to interest all who are anxious for information concerning the philosophy of which the author is such an able exponent."—*Times* Pittsburg, June, 1903.

"A glance over a few of its pages would be sufficient to convince the reader that he is in the presence of an intellect of high order, more thoroughly conversant with the philosophies and sciences of the Occidental world than most Europeans or Americans. . . . The "Divine Heritage of Man" gives a rare insight into the religious views of educated Hindoos and in its argumentation furnishes an intellectual treat."—*Chronicle*, San Francisco, Aug. 1903.

"Fully cognizant of modern scientific discoveries, the author treats his subject broadly."—*Bookseller, Newsdealer, and Publisher*, New York, Aug. 1903.

"The student of religions will find much of value in the discourses, since they are full of historical information concerning the origin and growth of certain ideas and beliefs dominant in Christianity."—*Republican*, Denver, July, 1903.

"There is no disposition on the part of the author to assail any of the Christian principles, but he simply presents his subject with calmness, not attempting to reconcile religion and science, for to him they are one."—*Washington Post*, June, 1903.

Self-Knowledge (Atma-Jnana).

BY SWAMI ABHEDANANDA

Cloth, $1.25. Postage, 8 cents. Portrait of author, frontispiece.

CONTENTS.

"So practically and exhaustively is each phase of the subject treated that it may well serve as a text-book for anyone striving for self-development and a deeper understanding of human nature." —*Toronto Saturday Night*, Dec. 1905.

"It will also be welcomed by students of the Vedic Scriptures, since each chapter is based upon some one of the ancient Vedas known as the Upanishads, and many passages are quoted."—*Chicago Inter-Ocean*, Jan. 1906.

"The book, from the gifted pen of the head of the Vedanta Society of New York, presents in a clear manner, calculated to arrest the attention of those not yet familiar with Vedic literature, the principles of self-knowledge as taught by the leaders of that philosophy. . . . The many passages quoted prove the profound wisdom and practical teaching contained in the early Hindu Scriptures."—*Washington Evening Star*, Dec. 1905.

"A new book which will be welcome to students of Truth, whether it be found in the Eastern religions, in modern thought or elsewhere."—*Unity*, Nov. 1905.

"The book is very well written."—*San Francisco Chronicle*, Dec. 1905.

"In forcefulness and clearness of style it is in every way equal to the other works by the Swami Abhedananda, who has always shown himself in his writings a remarkable master of the English language."—*Mexican Herald*, Dec. 1905.

"The volume is forcefully written, as are all of this author's works, and cannot fail to be of great interest to all who have entered this field of thought. A fine portrait of the Swami forms the frontispiece."—*Toledo Blade*, Nov. 1905.

PRESS NOTICES OF "INDIA AND HER PEOPLE."

"The views set forth in this work by Swami Abhedananda . . . are interesting, as being those of a native of India who has devoted much time and attention to the study of those questions which affect the government and general administration of the country. The author has selected a wide range of subjects for treatment, embracing the social, political, educational, and religious conditions as they now exist, and, speaking generally, has invariably exercised sound tact and judgment in discussing the many different questions embraced under those headings."—*Journal of the Royal Colonial Institute, April, 1907, London, England.*

"An excellent contribution to the very scanty literature on India. . . . All chapters are instructive to any one aspiring to a knowledge of this vast country. . . . It is a book which every non-Indian visiting India or making a temporary or permanent stay therein, and also every son of the soil, should have by his side."—*The Arya, February, 1907, Madras, India.*

Reincarnation.

(New and Enlarged Edition.)

I. Reincarnation.
II. Heredity and Reincarnation.
III. Evolution and Reincarnation.
IV. Which is Scientific, Resurrection or Reincarnation?
V. Theory of Transmigration.

Paper, 50 cents. Cloth, 75 cents. Postage, 5 and 7 cents.

"In these discourses the Swami Abhedananda considers the questions of evolution and the resurrection in their bearing upon the ancient teaching of rebirth, the truth, logic and justice of which are rapidly permeating the best thought of the Western world. For the preservation of this doctrine mankind is indebted to the literary storehouses of India, the racial and geographical source of much of the vital knowledge of Occidental peoples. Reincarnation is shown in the present volume to be a universal solvent of life's mysteries. It answers those questions of children that have staggered the wisest minds who seek to reconcile the law of evolution and the existence of an intelligent and just Creator, with the proposition that man has but a single lifetime in which to develop spiritual self-consciousness. It is commended to every thinker." —*Mind, February, 1900.*

"It is a work which will appeal to the novice for its simplicity and definite quality, and to the student for its wealth of knowledge and suggestion."—*Vedanta Monthly Bulletin, Sept., 1907.*

"The book should prove a valuable acquisition."—*The Evening Sun, N. Y., December 21, 1907.*

"This is the work of a man of fine education and of fine intellect. . . . (Reincarnation) as expounded by Swami Abhedananda is very plausible, quite scientific, and far from uncomforting. The exposition contained in this little book is well worth reading by all students of metaphysics. There is not the slightest danger of its converting or perverting any one to a new and strange religion. Reincarnation is not religion, it is science. Science was never known to hurt anybody but scientists."—*Brooklyn Eagle, December 13, 1907.*

WORKS BY SWÂMI ABHEDÂNANDA.

Philosophy of Work.

I. Philosophy of Work.
II. Secret of Work.
III. Duty or Motive in Work.

Paper, 50 cents. Cloth, 75 cents. Postage, 2 and 6 cents.

"In this volume the Vedanta Society presents three lectures by the leader of the Hindu religious movement that is making much headway among philosophic minds throughout the United States. The book is an excellent antidote to the gospel of selfism now popular in many quarters, and a copy should be in the hands especially of every ambitious seeker after the loaves and fishes of material desire. It shows the folly of slavery to sense and the means of escape from the thraldom of egoism, while elucidating the Hindu concept of many things that are 'race problems' because of individual ignorance of spiritual principles. These discourses merit a wide circulation among unprejudiced minds."—*Mind*, February, 1903.

Single Lectures.

CHRISTIAN SCIENCE AND VEDANTA.
COSMIC EVOLUTION AND ITS PURPOSE.
DIVINE COMMUNION.
DOES THE SOUL EXIST AFTER DEATH?
THE MOTHERHOOD OF GOD.
THE PHILOSOPHY OF GOOD AND EVIL.
THE RELATION OF SOUL TO GOD.
RELIGION OF THE HINDUS.
SCIENTIFIC BASIS OF RELIGION.
SIMPLE LIVING.
SPIRITUALISM AND VEDANTA.
THE WAY TO THE BLESSED LIFE.
WHO IS THE SAVIOUR OF SOULS?
WHY A HINDU ACCEPTS CHRIST AND REJECTS CHURCHIANITY.
WHY A HINDU IS A VEGETARIAN.
WOMAN'S PLACE IN HINDU RELIGION.
THE WORD AND THE CROSS IN ANCIENT INDIA.

15 cents each. Postage, 2 cents each.

Single Lectures Parts I & II. Bound in cloth, each $1.25. Postage, 8 cents.

The Sayings of Sri Râmakrishna.

COMPILED BY

SWÂMI ABHEDÂNANDA.

234 pages. Flexible cloth, gilt top, $1.00. Postage, 6c.

Râmakrishna was a great Hindu saint of the nineteenth century who has already had an influence on the religious thought of America and England through the teachings of his disciples, Swâmi Vivekânanda, Swâmi Abhedânanda, and others. His Sayings are full of broad, practical, non-sectarian instructions concerning the spiritual life which cannot but give help and inspiration to the followers of all creeds. The present volume contains a larger number of Sayings than has yet appeared in any one English collection. For the first time also they have been classified into chapters and arranged in logical sequence under marginal headings, such as "All creeds paths to God," "Power of Mind and Thought," "Meditation," "Perseverance." As an exposition of the universal truths of Religion and their application to the daily life this book takes its place among the great scriptures of the world.

Spiritual Unfoldment.

BY SWAMI ABHEDANANDA

I. Self-control.
II. Concentration and Meditation.
III. God-consciousness.

Paper, 50 cents. Cloth, 75 cents. Postage, 2 and 6 cents.

"This attractive little volume comprises three lectures on the Vedanta Philosophy. The discourses will be found vitally helpful even by those who know little and care less about the spiritual and ethical teachings of which the Swami is an able and popular exponent. As the Vedanta itself is largely a doctrine of universals and ultimates, so also is this book of common utility and significance among all races of believers. Its precepts are susceptible of application by any rational thinker, regardless of religious predilection and inherited prejudices. The principles set forth by this teacher are an excellent corrective of spiritual bias or narrowness, and as such the present work is to be commended. It has already awakened an interest in Oriental literature that augurs well for the cause of human brotherhood, and it merits a wide circulation among all who cherish advanced ideals."—*Mind, April, 1902.*

What is Vedanta?

Pamphlet printed for distribution containing a short exposition of the fundamental teachings of the Vedanta Philosophy. 12mo, 8 pp. Price, 10 cents.